How EMDR* Therapy Transformed My Life

*Eye Movement Desensitization Reprocessing

From *"God Hole"* to *"God Whole"*

Marie Pflugrad

World rights reserved. This book or any portion thereof may not be copied or reproduced in any form or manner whatever, except as provided by law, without the written permission of the publisher, except by a reviewer who may quote brief passages in a review.

"I have tried to recreate events, locales, and conversations from my memories of them. In order to maintain their anonymity, I have changed the names of individuals and places, in some instances, and I may have changed some identifying characteristics and details such as physical properties, occupations, and places of residence."

All scriptures quoted in this book are from *The Holy Bible, New King James Version*, copyright 1979, 1980, 1982, HarperCollins. Used by permission of Thomas Nelson Publishers.

Copyright © 2020 Marie Pflugrad

Copyright © 2020 TEACH Services, Inc.

ISBN-13: 978-1-4796-1161-4 (Paperback)

ISBN-13: 978-1-4796-1162-1 (ePub)

Library of Congress Control Number: 2020900135

Acknowledgement

I marvel at clichés like "There's no place like home" or "home is where the heart is". In the process of writing this book I've come to realize that as the wife of a pastor, I will likely not have a permanent home for any great length of time here on this earth. I'm fine with that, given the fact that this world is not my real home anyway. I long for the day when I'll have my permanent home with Jesus. So, in acknowledging Jesus, I would say that "Jesus is where the heart is". He has made His home in my heart. So, I first and foremost want to acknowledge Him. My Creator and Healer. The One who has shown me love when others have failed me. He has taught me forgiveness and continues to teach me, and He places people and situations in my path for specific reasons. I will be forever grateful to Him. It is, after all God who has given me all things, including the following people who I would also like to acknowledge:

My precious husband Terry, who has been my steady supporter for the past thirteen years. His love and comfort in going through some of the darkest periods of my life were critical to my healing process. His continuous reminders that "this is temporary, you can get through this". His love, faith, prayers and strong connection to God gave me the strength and desire to believe there truly is hope for a happier existence. He never stopped encouraging me to keep writing. He never gave up on me and he stuck by my side when many men would have run the other direction. You are the most wonderful husband a woman could hope to find and I will love you forever. Thank you for accepting me, faults and all.

I would also like to acknowledge the two therapist who facilitated my healing process of Post Traumatic Stress Disorder (PTSD) with Complex Trauma. Their expertise in using EMDR (Eye Movement Desensitization Reprocessing) therapy was essential. Without their patient, kind, and compassionate care, I seriously doubt the healing could have taken place. Ronald R. Baptist (MA, LPC, EMDRIA Certified Approved Consultant) who treated me in Colorado and his amazing wife Beverly, who went the extra mile. Ron (with Beverly as his right hand) rearranged his schedule countless times to fit me in during times of crisis. His faith in God and willingness to pray for me when I asked him to, did not go unrecognized. Thank you for being blunt with me and pulling no punches. Your firm, yet caring approach was what I needed. Your strong belief in EMDR convinced me that I could benefit from it and I'm so glad I listened to you! Thank you for tirelessly working to bring healing to so many! I will always appreciate you and Bev. I no longer fear spiders! Thank you for that.

Lynnea Ritz (MSW, LCSW, EMDRIA Certified Approved Consultant, EMDR Consulting Training Coach), you are a wonderful, cheerful Christian woman and I appreciate you so much. Thank you for helping me process some of the most gut-wrenching realizations that came out during my therapy sessions. I feel I owe you a few boxes of tissues! Thank you for loaning me the books that opened my eyes to so much truth about EMDR. And for Oggie, your therapy dog who would sit at my feet and sometimes lay next to me. He was a soothing, inviting part of each session.

It is very important for me to acknowledge Dr. Francine Shapiro who was the founder of EMDR therapy and the EMDR Institute. Without her knowledge and the God given gifts she received, many of us would not be receiving the help and healing that she has brought to the world. It is with sadness that Francine passed away on June 16, 2019 at the age of 71. She leaves behind an amazing legacy that is unending. While I did not personally know Dr. Shapiro, I recently had the opportunity to talk to her personal friend, and the Administrative director of the EMDR Institute, Robbie Dunton. The reason for my reaching out to Robbie, was that I wanted to acknowledge Dr. Shapiro in this book and I felt I needed to know more about Francine on a personal level rather than merely as a clinician. Robbie really helped me to see the precious human side of Francine. She gave me permission to print an excerpt from the tribute she gave in honor of Francine at the EMDRIA conference in September 2019. This is what she shared:

In the approximately 36+ years I was fortunate to have known her, she shared her love of Mother Teresa, roses, music, dancing, traveling, dogs, children, horses, dark chocolate, baklava, Buddha statues, and wandering in nature, especially along the cliffs above the beach- a daily source of inspiration and joy for her. Her involvement in spirituality and the teachings of Judaism were very important parts of her life. Most of all, she loved her life's work to healing the world with EMDR therapy.

I share a couple of the websites that are available regarding EMDR in the chapter titled "What is EMDR? I strongly encourage you to look at these if you have any questions or want more information on the topic and on the works of Dr. Francine Shapiro. I will be forever grateful to Dr. Shapiro for her discovery of such an amazing healing methodology.

In closing, I would like to acknowledge TEACH Services for helping me with all that goes in to writing a book. This is my first endeavor and I have found it to be a fun adventure. Also, thank you to those who love and support me and have been there for me through every phase of my life so far. You know who you are and I am forever indebted to each and every one of you.

"Aha" and Notes pages: I encourage you to jot down notes or "Aha moments" on the blank pages provided in this book. In the event that something jumps out at you while you're reading, that resonate with you so you can reference it at a later time.

Thank you for reading this book and my prayer is that you will be blessed.

Marie

"Marie's compelling story of redemption from a life that began without much of any love, support, or caring, is a testament to the power of God to break through any deficits in our life and redeem even the ugliest of disadvantages. It also speaks volumes of Marie—that she would have the desire to keep exploring painful memories and hurts until she reached the unvarnished truth—all with the hope that healing would come.

"Her story also reminds us that it does no harm whatsoever to Divine power, one's faith, and personal tenacity to seek the help of a qualified, Christian therapist who can help us discover what's really at the root of our self-view and how to find healing where it's needed.

"Thank you, Marie, for your courage in sharing your powerful story with us! It's my hope that it can catalyze others to believe that they, too, can be God Whole."

—Mic Thurber, Ministerial Director, Mid-America Union Conference

"This book traces the author's journey from brokenness, rejection, and dysfunction to hope, healing, and wholeness. It is frank, honest, and vulnerable as it addresses the hard issues of abuse, addiction, and neglect. It chronicles what it is like to feel unwanted and unloved or at best, loved only conditionally. While it openly acknowledges the sin problem, it does not glorify the condition which we all find ourselves a part of. The principles underlying the therapy used appear rooted in the value that Heaven places on every individual. It resonates with Christ's words in John 8:32, 'the truth shall make you free.'

"The author does a good job of articulating her thoughts and emotions but with a constant eye toward what God has done and what He is still doing in her experience. It is a practical look at what can happen in the life of one who is willing to commit themselves fully to God while being willing to do the hard work of recovery. It is a useful resource for those who may struggle with similar issues but it can apply to almost anyone 'willing to hear it' since we are all wounded and damaged by being in a sinful world.

"It is interesting that research referenced in the book confirms a statement made many years ago by a favorite author of mine... 'She (a mother), by whose lifeblood the child is nourished and its physical frame built up, imparts to it also mental and spiritual influences that tend to the shaping of mind and character' (MH 372)."

—Merlin Knowles, Ministerial Secretary, Dakota Conference

"I highly recommend this powerful, and resourceful, read if you are searching for the truth in regard to God's love for you and the infinite possibilities He has in store for you. Possibilities that Satan (the enemy) so desperately wants to keep hidden!

I have personally known the author for nearly thirty years. Her passion for Jesus and ability to connect with children and adults who share similar experiences qualifies her to provide the reader with encouragement and pertinent information. Her personal journey of healing is a must read.

—Carlene Lang, Educator, Kansas-Nebraska Conference

"Armed with a master's degree in teaching, Marie is alarmed when a five-year-old's screaming sparks long-suppressed memories of her own childhood abuse. This book powerfully depicts the anguish and struggle required to climb to wholeness through the acceptance of God's unconditional love and the use of Eye Movement Desensitization Reprocessing (EMDR). This is an educational, informational, and an enjoyable read."

—Jacqueline Biloff, Communication Director, Dakota Conference

Table of Contents

CHAPTER 1 : How It All Began 11
CHAPTER 2 : A Blast from the Past 19
CHAPTER 3 : Where I Came From: Mom's History 25
CHAPTER 4 : Where I Came From: Dad's History 34
CHAPTER 5 : First Marriage...43
CHAPTER 6 : My Do Over 53
CHAPTER 7 : What is EMDR?...59
CHAPTER 8 : Am I Loveable?..67
CHAPTER 9 : Conditional Love...73
CHAPTER 10 : More Tragic Memories 79
CHAPTER 11 : Letter to Mom 87
CHAPTER 12 : Forced to Be Tough...97
CHAPTER 13 : Mom's Death 107
CHAPTER 14 : Breakthrough Therapy Session....................................116
CHAPTER 15 : My Last Letter..124
CHAPTER 16 : Final Thoughts from the Author 130

Chapter 1

How It All Began

Who am I? I thought to myself, pondering the question. A short summary came to mind. I consider myself a fairly intelligent woman in my fifties, who had been a schoolteacher for over twenty years, a divorcee with two grown sons, and now the wife of a pastor, who enjoyed my role in visiting parishioners and helping with Bible studies. I like to sing, play the guitar, bake, and substitute teach on occasion. Did I mention that I'm in my fifties?

I'm stunned that I could possibly be this old! Where has the time gone? I thought to myself. A mirror hanging on the wall revealed a square-jawed woman with dishwater blonde bangs, framing a face topped off by wire-rimmed glasses. Long, straight hair hung behind the shoulders of a somber but kind looking green-eyed woman peering back at me. I looked myself over and then, as I turned my head to the left, the scar on the right side of my face glared at me. It was the shape of a "J," or fishhook, about two and a half inches in length.

As if little snippets of a movie reel quickly flashing, a rush of memories rolled before my mind's eye. Self-analysis of what took place over the years had led me to the waiting room of a licensed Clinical Social Worker. Another trauma therapy session was just ahead. I was on a quest for healing, and I had no choice but to start at the very beginning. I had to explore where it all began.

In short, I am a recovering alcoholic with over 30 years of sobriety under my belt. *Wow! An alcoholic! Sober that long!* My eyebrows furrowed in a look of puzzlement. *Why would that thought come to my mind first, when describing myself?* While being an alcoholic does not define me and drinking hasn't been a part of my life for decades, I couldn't help but think about the first time I remember being exposed to liquor. I was saddened in thinking about the key role that alcohol had played in my early life and how different things could have been.

I suddenly drifted back in time and remembered my older brothers having my sister and me drink that nasty tasting liquid when we were just toddlers. My dad kept a couple of bottles in the kitchen cupboard, and he would take a swig at midnight to bring in the New Year each December 31st. Jim Beam, Wild Turkey, and Southern Comfort were his favorites. Other than that, I never saw my dad drink anything other than water, milk, coffee, and Dr. Pepper. My brothers obviously knew where Daddy's stash was.

On that particular night, my parents were apparently gone, and my twin sister and I were being babysat by our older siblings, consisting of three brothers and an older sister. I remember them making me drink it. It was horrible, and it made me choke. It burned my throat. Yet, with each numbing swallow, it became easier to take. I remember how they laughed as I staggered through the living room. My sister and I were both naked, and I remember my sister putting my dad's cowboy boots on and trying to run. She tripped and fell, and the boys laughed. I took a turn putting the boots on, and I also fell and stumbled about. I remember the feeling of frustration, embarrassment, and shame, while still wanting to please my siblings with entertainment and laughter. It was, as I think back, a confusing feeling. As far back as I can remember, I always wanted to please people, and I can recall being told, "Keep your mouth shut!" I heard those words quite often as a child.

> *I took a turn putting the boots on, and I also fell and stumbled about. I remember the feeling of frustration, embarrassment, and shame, while still wanting to please my siblings with entertainment and laughter*

While neither of my parents were drinkers, beer was always available. By the time I was ten, I was stealing full and even half empty cans from the back of my older brother's pickup truck. It was my secret, and I carefully kept it under "lock and key." I couldn't wait for my brother to come home after being out partying with his friends. I looked forward to the challenge of sneaking into the pickup bed to see how much I could take. I was disappointed whenever I found nothing but empty cardboard boxes.

I recall a couple of times when I visited my dad's whiskey "stash" in the kitchen cupboard. I poured the dark brown liquid into a glass and, paying close attention to how much I had taken, filled the stolen amount of liquid with water as a replacement. I took pride in my clever endeavor to hide my thievery so Daddy wouldn't notice the bottles' contents missing. I stealthily snuck my container to the upstairs room and drank it. There was an instant, out-of-body feeling I can vividly remember, which had an escape quality. Even now, in thinking back to that time, I find it hard to define the rush of feelings—the fear and exhilaration all at the same time. This was the beginning of my addictive behaviors, the beginning of my need to numb my emotions.

When I was in the sixth grade, a new girl moved to our town. Her name was Carla, and she was in my class. We became fast friends. Her dad was a Vietnam veteran and a heavy drinker. On numerous occasions, I was allowed to ride the bus home with her to stay the weekend. My parents really didn't know her parents and didn't even ask about them. It seemed as if my mom was just glad to have me out of the house.

I'll never forget my nervousness on that cold November Friday. I had stolen two twenty-four-ounce cans of Coors beer (also known as "tall boys") from my brother's pickup, which I smuggled to school in my winter coat. I put one can down each sleeve and snapped the cuff shut as tight as I could. I hung the coat up on the peg in the back of the classroom where it stayed all day. As the day dragged on and on, I kept one eye on the teacher and the other on the row of coats. I volunteered to stay in for recess so I wouldn't have to go outside and put on my puffy goose down jacket. I couldn't let that coat out of my sight, and I felt like a jealous dog guarding a bone. What a relief it was when the teacher told us to line up for the bus at the end of the day. I cradled my coat across my arm and squeezed the ends of the cuffs securely so the beer couldn't fall out. With my backpack and friend in tow, we headed to the bus so we could sneak off and drink the coveted beer without interruption. Nobody noticed, and we were never found out.

The drive-in theater and roller-skating rink were the most popular hangouts for my friends and me. By the time I was in middle school, my mom was nearing fifty and was eager to have the last of her kids gone. Looking back, I can see that she had pretty much checked out of the parenting job. She enjoyed her career as the administrative assistant to the local district attorney, and she was probably just naïve about what her teenage twin daughters were doing. But, then again, I don't remember her ever asking questions. She said she "trusted" me. But I was never worthy of trust. Looking back, I believe my mom had unconcerned indifference for her children. It seemed to me that she just never cared.

Most Fridays I would call Mom at work to tell her where I would be staying for the weekend. I didn't really ask her; I just told her. I had at least four friends that I could rotate my weekend to stay with. At age 14, I was attending keggers (parties where kegs of beer sat on tailgates). Beer was unlimited and had been purchased by the older kids I hung out with.

In the 1980s, beer that contained a 3.2% alcohol level was legal for purchase in Colorado for those who were eighteen or older. Beer containing 6% alcohol was restricted to those twenty-one years old or older. Suffice it to say, it wasn't difficult finding booze. I became so good at lying to my parents about my whereabouts that they didn't even try to find me.

My risky behavior even went on under my parents own roof and on their property. Because our ranch was ten miles outside of town, it wasn't as convenient for my friends to stay with me. However, on one particular occasion, I invited a friend over for the weekend. We had made plans for an older relative to make a beer delivery for us. We promised—on pain of death—never to reveal his identity. He was to drop off a case of beer along the road near a specified place that we could retrieve later that evening. We told my parents we were going to stay the night down in the sand gulch where we had made a make-shift fort. It was a hot summer evening, and they agreed. As soon as it was dusk, we headed to the drop off point. Sure enough, there it was! I'll never forget how drunk we got. We laughed so hard I wet my pants. We told stories, played games, and drank beer. But, oh, did we ever have a hangover!

While my twin sister and I had many of the same friends, I saw her as a tag-along. I was more adventurous and established my own identity at an early age. When I wanted something, I went for it. I wanted to play the guitar so badly that I taught myself how by watching Mac Davis on his television program. For $20.00, I bought an old student guitar from my sister-in-law, and I sat and drew pictures of where Mac Davis put his fingers on the neck of his guitar. My dad played the guitar, and he gave me pointers from time to time. My older sister, who took a guitar class in school, shared a few guitar tips with me too.

For hours on end, I would hide away upstairs, making up lyrics and tunes to go along with them. My twin was shy and resented my wanting her to sing with me. The only thing she seemed interested in were her Barbie dolls. Once I felt confident enough with a few songs, I took my guitar along with me for weekend parties, and those of us who played the guitar would sing and drink, and drink and sing. I'm sure it was quite a cacophony of sounds, but we thought we were good. By age fourteen, I had written over thirty songs.

I attempted to smoke my first cigarette with a cousin when I was nine, but I didn't learn to inhale until Carla came to town during my sixth-grade year. By eleven, I was smoking every cigarette I could get my hands on. I hung out with the older kids in my 4-H club who were smokers, so starting smoking just seemed like a natural progression. Middle school was where my circle of friends enlarged, and marijuana was easily obtained. Being a ranch kid, however, I equated marijuana with the hippie crowd, and I wanted nothing to do with them. I'm thankful for not getting addicted to that horrible habit. My habits were bad enough as it was.

When I was fifteen, I had a huge crush on a fellow 4-H member. He was three years older than I was and was legal to drink. We went out on a few dates and partied regularly, but he was interested in another girl. I was devastated when he dumped me. Feeling rejected and vulnerable, I allowed myself to get involved with a guy fresh out of the Navy. He was a muscular, charismatic, divorced 22-year-old man with two young daughters. He knew exactly what to say to a naive 16-year-old country girl. He lured me in with his manipulation and flattering compliments over the next three years. His best friend was even smoother than he was. He charmed my twin sister right down the aisle. They were married when she was seventeen and still a senior in high school. Graduating, and on the honor roll, she seemed to have found her niche. She couldn't wait to become a wife and "Becky home maker." My sister's new independence gave us a legitimate place to party. It was no longer weekends on dirt roads and abandoned campsites. I now had access to hard liquor.

By age sixteen, I had a job at one of the local burger joints, so I did make some money. However, most of my paychecks went toward beer, cigarettes, and gasoline for my old Ford Galaxy 500. Oddly enough, I did value my education, and I wanted to get my high school diploma. I was drinking every night, but I still showed up for school. I fell asleep during the morning classes and my teacher complained to administration, and administration called my parents. I remember my mom lecturing me as I walked out the door. My only response was a disrespectful eye roll. She didn't seem concerned about me but was only peeved that I would dare to bring embarrassment upon her.

My mom detested my Navy boyfriend and told me that I should dump him. She didn't give me reasons; she just didn't like him, which inevitably caused me to like him more. I did see red flags, and my gut told me he was all wrong. We had nothing in common, and it was strictly a physical attraction. I caught him in some lies, and, when I confronted him, he became abusive. In my frail state, I couldn't escape him, and the abuse went on for over two years. He would cheat on me and then beat on me. Then I would receive a dozen beautiful roses with the sweetest apology, begging his forgiveness. This became a routine and quite predictable, but as a 17-year-old who had been brainwashed and convinced that no one else could possibly want me, I was glad to have him back. He was so methodical in his abuse that he could somehow make me believe that I deserved to be beaten and tortured and that he was doing me a favor by *letting* me be with him. He convinced me that my beatings were my own fault. He would cry as I sat there bleeding and say things like, "Look what you made me do!" Needless to say, my binge drinking went to an all-time high.

By the time I was eighteen, I was a full-blown alcoholic with the liver of a 65-year-old. At least that's what the doctor told me at my initial evaluation when I admitted myself into a 30-day alcohol treatment facility. The events of the evening that led up to my entering treatment haunt me to this day.

> *I was so sorry that I had hurt him. He walked me back into the house and held me while I cried*

I had come home extremely drunk and my parents were waiting up for me. I immediately got into an argument with my mom. When my dad tried to get my car keys from me, I took off my leather belt, which had a large, heavy buckle on the end, and I began swinging it around my head at my dad. I struck him a couple times, and, when I saw the look of hurt on his face and the blood running down the side of his head, I fell to the ground crying. I was so sorry that I had hurt him. He walked me back into the house and held me while I cried. I begged him to get me help, and the next day I was being driven to a chemical dependency unit in Pueblo, Colorado.

I took the treatment very seriously and worked the 30-day program pretty well for an 18-year-old. Looking back today, however, I recognize that while the Alcoholics Anonymous program has a spiritual component to it, I still didn't get it. I didn't really know how to pray or how to find God. Yet, I sensed His presence in my heart and mind, and I had a genuine desire to know Him better. I did understand the 12-step program on an intellectual basis, and the first of those steps was a blatant truth that I couldn't deny. I readily accepted step 1: *I admitted that I was powerless over alcohol—that my life had become unmanageable.* No problem with that one! It was just a fact.

Step 2 was a bit of a challenge because I had lost hope. Step 2 says: *Came to believe that a Power greater than myself could restore me to sanity.* It would take faith to buy into this step, and I didn't really understand what *faith* meant. I certainly didn't want to admit *insanity!*

Step 3 says: *Made a decision to turn my will and my life over to the care of God as I understand Him.* This was without a doubt the most challenging step! I got bogged down in it. First of all, *"as I understood Him?"* I didn't understand who God is. I didn't have a healthy picture of God or of Jesus. Somehow, though, I had a sense of who the Holy Spirit was, so I clung to Him. I listened for that still small voice, and I talked to Whoever that was.

I managed to stay sober for eleven months. I attended AA meetings and decided to go back to church. The abusive boyfriend found greener pastures as my new-found spiritual awakening made me far less appealing to him. The Lutheran church I grew up in had relocated, and I wasn't comfortable going there anyway. So, I attended the Baptist, Methodist, and Evangelical Free churches to see if I fit in. None seemed right for me. It was when I stepped into the Pentecostal church and was expected to start speaking in tongues that I decided to take a break from church shopping.

I took a job at an electronics plant and found some new friends who were supportive of my new-found sobriety. I moved out of my parents' home, and a friend and I rented a mobile home in a local trailer park. We shared all expenses, and now I had complete freedom. I even bought my first car. It was a shiny 1978 red 2-door Ford Pinto. It was my pride and joy.

Chapter Notes and "Aha" Moments :

Chapter 2

A Blast from the Past

Then, out of nowhere, *he* came back. It was Satan himself, cloaked under the cover of my old boyfriend. He was full of promises that he had changed. "I just can't live without you," he said. I should have listened to the still, small voice within, but, once again, my need to be loved and my fear of rejection won over, and there I was again—back to his beck and call, and back to the bottle where I could numb myself from his cruelty.

One day after I got off work, I was heading to my car, when I noticed a folded piece of paper lying on my seat. *Oh, a love-note*, I thought to myself. But it wasn't a love note. Instead, it was a note from my mom.

> *Dear Marie,*
>
> *I know you are seeing "him" again, and I am worried about you. He is the devil himself, and you need to stay as far away from him as you can.*
>
> *Mom*

I remember crumpling the note up and throwing it in my back seat. I was so infatuated with him, and I was so angry that my mom would do such a thing. Somehow, I wanted to believe that he really did love me. I had now ignored the still small voice and the advice of my mom. What was it going to take to get me to end this relationship?

> ***I should have listened to the still, small voice within, but, once again, my need to be loved and my fear of rejection won over, and there I was again—back to his beck and call, and back to the bottle where I could numb myself from his cruelty***

And then it happened—his mistake would prove to be my escape route. He had lied to me for the last time, and he could not cover it up or run away from it.

The receiver of the pay phone was chilly next to my face as I listened to the ring on the other end. It was a cold October evening, or, rather, morning, for it was 2:00 a.m. by the time I made the call. I had been out driving all night. It was my usual routine to get a case of beer and go for a road trip when I was upset or happy—or for basically any reason. My eleven months of sobriety had slipped away as a complete failure, and I had driven the last two hours, in my lonely despair, trying to locate my boyfriend whom I was supposed to have met at 10:00 p.m.

I had my suspicions of where he might be. He had a way of hiding his car, though, so I decided to call the house of the woman I thought he might be sneaking around with.

What a shock it was when he answered her phone. "So, you are there?" I screamed into the cold receiver, my breath heavy with steam and alcohol.

"Don't you ever call me here again!" he retorted. Then, there was a pause, and I could tell that he had moved to another location.

"Are you in bed with her now?" I questioned accusatorily with hostility in my voice.

"Yes, but she means nothing to me. ... I love you!" My shock and confusion rose to a higher level as I screamed a few choice expletives at him.

"Then why are you there?" I demanded.

There was a long pause before his answer, which felt like a kick in the stomach, when he said, "She's pregnant; you and I are done. You need to leave me alone and stay out of my life."

Instead of jumping for joy and seeing this as my perfect way out of hell, I began to cry. I sobbed and just let the phone fall. It seemed at that very moment that my life was over. My rejection was complete. Even a sick, abusive, two-timing cheat didn't want me. How much lower could I have possibly felt?

I got into my car and headed north on a two-lane road. I was doing about 80 miles per hour when I came to a tight corner at the top of the hill. My rock music was deafening, and I had decided that there was no point in living any more. I spun my steering wheel as hard as I could as I hit the corner and the gravel. Time stood still, and it was as if my life played out before me. Only seconds passed, yet it seemed like an eternity. I saw the panorama of my life—faces of people I knew and blinks of segments of time—flash through my mind. Then, came the crash. The car was facing the opposite direction, and it began to flip. I remember smashing sounds and loud music. My cassette player was still screaming out a "Molly Hatchet" tune. Then there was a loud thump and a jolting stop, as everything suddenly stood still in complete blackness.

I instinctively reached for the door handle to get out of my car, and it came off in my hand. I was in a sitting position, but I was not in my seat. There was glass broken under my feet, and I looked down between my legs to see my dome light. I was sitting in my upturned car with the bucket seats above my head. I reached for the window handle to roll it down so I could get out, and it broke off as well. Everything was the reverse of what it should have been. I finally kicked the passenger window and got it to shatter. Then I climbed through the broken window and stood up. There was a strange tickling sensation on my face. I reached up and felt a warm liquid oozing down my cheek.

I had landed near the driveway of an elderly couple that my family knew. I learned later that the actual yard where I landed was the home of a deputy in the sheriff's department. I believe now that God's divine intervention led me to walk to the front door of the house of that sweet elderly couple. I had to climb a fairly steep bank and a concrete wall to get to their house, but I was compelled to get to it. I rang the doorbell. When the door opened, I was met by the horrified couple. They quickly pulled me into the house and closed the door.

"Put the coffee pot on, Eva," I heard the man say to his wife.

"Have you had a little bit to drink tonight?" he asked me.

"Just a little," I answered. "My car is outside on its top," I said, with a bit of a slur.

"Oh, I'll go take a look."

With that, he went out into the night. Eva came into the room, and I still had my hand on my face. She grew pale as she noticed the blood.

"Let me take a look at your face, dear," she said, as she walked closer to me. I didn't realize it at the time, but I could practically put three fingers inside my face. The laceration was gaping open and blood was running down my arm.

"I'm so sorry," I sobbed, as I looked down at the blood dripping on her floor. She quickly retreated to the kitchen and rushed back with a towel and held it to my face.

"Here, put some pressure on that," she instructed. I leaned back in the chair and closed my eyes for a bit. She began mopping the blood off the linoleum floor.

The door slowly opened as Irwin came back into the house. "I turned your car off and the headlights too," he called. "You need to give her another cup of coffee, Honey," he instructed, as she rounded the corner. I didn't realize it at the time, but he was trying to sober me up before he made a phone call.

I fell asleep in the chair after about the third cup of coffee. When I awoke, I heard the man talking in a low, muffled voice in the next room, but I couldn't make out the conversation. What seemed like hours, was only two.

The next thing I knew, my mom was standing in the doorway. Irwin had called her, and she came to take me to the hospital. I had no desire to talk to my mom. She was clearly upset but not that I had been hurt. She seemed inconvenienced. I remember wishing my dad had come and not her. Daddy couldn't stand being in hospitals because of his childhood experience, so I had to deal with my mom.

> *I awoke to a Highway Patrol officer just inches from my face. He was obviously trying to get a sniff of my breath*

I awoke to a Highway Patrol officer just inches from my face. He was obviously trying to get a sniff of my breath. My eyes opened, startling him. He stepped back and asked if I could answer a few questions for him. My face was aching, and I was stiff all over. I learned that I had a slight concussion and that I needed over 100 stitches in my face, internal and external. The cut was in the shape of a J, or a fishhook, just in front of my right ear.

"What happened last night?" the officer asked.

In my ever-so-nimble ability to cover my tracks, I simply stated, "I was coming up the hill on Dozier Avenue, and there was a car coming at me in my lane with his lights on bright. I swerved to avoid a head on, and I must have over corrected. The next thing I knew, I was off the cliff."

Tapping his note pad and nodding his head, he told me he would write up his report. "Get some rest, and heal up," he said, as he reached for the door of the hospital room. The patrolman and my mom knew each other, and they visited for a while before he left. Something always made me feel that he knew I had been drinking but was doing my mom a favor by not giving me a ticket or by prodding further.

I went home with my mom so someone could monitor my concussion for the next couple of days. There was never a ticket issued and no more follow-up visits from the patrolman. I had to pay $200.00 to replace a couple of trees my car destroyed as it crashed through the sheriff deputy's driveway. My car was a total loss, but the insurance company gave me a check to cover the value. $1,500.00 was put toward a 1978 baby blue Oldsmobile Cutlass Supreme with 150 thousand miles—my new car.

I went back to my trailer house and rested up for a few days before going back to work. It gave me time to reflect on everything that had just happened. I knew I had to make some serious changes. I needed to get to an AA meeting as soon as possible. Maybe I needed to look at finding a church to attend. No matter what, I vowed I would never allow that toxic, abusive man back into my life, and I was true to my word. Four months later, his new girlfriend gave birth to a baby boy—the spitting image of his daddy.

It might be helpful to know more about my mother and her background. Perhaps this will establish a better understanding of who I am and where I came from by shedding some light on our unique relationship.

Chapter Notes and "Aha" Moments :

Chapter 3

Where I Came From: Mom's History

I can hardly share things about my mother without backing up and giving a history of her beginnings. Part of the intrigue of generational curses is that they have a beginning somewhere, and my mother definitely had an interesting upbringing.

My maternal grandfather was just a boy when his parents came to America. He was born July 29, 1902 in Lindornerfeldt, Germany, which no longer exists today. His family had previously immigrated to the United States and purchased land in Iowa and Nebraska, so his parents settled in Nebraska. My grandmother was born in Harlan, Iowa, on July 3, 1907, and her parents were also immigrants from Europe. My grandparents met and were married in Logan, Iowa, on September 9, 1926. The majority of my information comes from the stories that my mother, grandmother, and aunts and uncles shared with me over the course of thirty-five years. I also found information written in Bibles that were left behind.

Grandpa was a staunch German who spoke his native language fluently but only spoke it to his relatives and my grandmother. My mom recalled her parents speaking in German when they didn't want the kids to know what they were saying. During heated discussions, he would speak in his native tongue, and Mom said he got very loud when he was angry. She said Grandpa refused to allow the children to speak German at all. He said that, as Americans, they were to forget their German heritage. After all, his kids were born on American soil, and they were to only speak English. My mom remembered some German words, however, and I was often called "dummkopf," which meant "stupid," or, literally, "blockhead." I'm certain that she had been called this by her parents too. Grandpa John wanted to forget Germany, and he hated being linked to what was going on during the war in his homeland.

My grandma was a small woman who cowered before her loud husband who barked orders and expected perfection from all who resided under the roof that he ruled with an iron fist. He was a chain smoker and rolled his own cigarettes. My mom recalled how the smoke billowed around his head as he lit one right off the other. He had a barking cough that made his voice rattle, and he stunk like old tobacco. He wasn't a tall man but only of average height. He was blocky, solidly built, and very strong, with broad shoulders and very large hands. He had a distinct widow's peak on his sandy blonde hair line and a very broad forehead. Most black and white photos show him in denim bib overalls. He rarely smiled, and, in most photos, he had a somber look with creases in his forehead. Mom said he had very blue eyes.

> *In those days, there was no term for "dysfunctional family." People were tough; they were strong; they were survivors—especially Germans*

My grandparents moved the family from Buck Grove, Iowa, to Colorado in 1937 so that Grandpa could work in the coal mines. My mom was seven years old at the time. She left behind her friends, her cousins, her pets, and her memories. They left in January, and she vividly remembered the freezing cold drive in their old Model-T Ford. She told me that she didn't understand why they left, but she alluded to the fact that it was not a very happy place nor was her childhood a happy one.

Because of the Great Depression, hardship was everywhere, and, even if a child were in an abusive home, no one thought to question it. In those days, there was no term for "dysfunctional family." People were tough; they were strong; they were survivors—especially Germans. They took pride in their heritage as having more resiliency than other nationalities. Children and women were voiceless, and what went on in the home, behind closed doors, was nobody else's business. There were mute skeletons in many closets back then.

Grandma had been deceased several years before my mom shared with me some of the things her mom had told her. Grandma didn't really want to marry Grandpa. She found out about his temper and was afraid of him. Yet, they were married in 1926. Within two months of being married, she wanted to leave him, but she discovered that she was already pregnant. Her dad had died in 1924 when she was only 18. She was very close to her mom, and her mom helped her with her new baby boy. Divorce was nearly unheard of back then, and she resigned herself to stay with him. My mom was born two years later, in 1929; then my mom's sister came two years after that. My great-grandmother Mary ended up moving with them to Colorado in 1937 and stayed until her death in 1961 at the age of 96. My mom loved her grandmother and said that she would stand up to her dad, whereas her own mother would not.

Child protective services did not exist in the 1930s. People were just trying to survive. My mom was an obedient child, by her own account. She admitted that she was afraid of her dad. Her older brother was their dad's pride and joy. Uncle Dale could do no wrong, and Grandpa was very lenient with him. Aunt Mae was my mother's younger sister. She was born with a cleft palate. She was called a "hair lip" because of her nasal tone, though she had no scar on her lip. She was shy, withdrawn, frail, and sickly. Grandpa was very cruel to Aunt Mae and insisted that she "talk right." According to Mom, Grandpa would yell at her and tell her that she could talk right if she would just try harder. He belittled her and accused her of talking "funny" just to get attention. He resented her and her impediment.

Aunt Mae grew up but never really did grow up. She never had a boyfriend, never dated, and never learned to drive a car. She was the epitome of a lonely old spinster. She lived with my grandmother well into her late thirties. I still remember the excitement when she bought her own home and moved into it with her little chihuahua, "Mitzi." It sat on her lap and ate from her plate at mealtime. Aunt Mae worked in the laundry of a nursing home just blocks from where she lived so she could walk to work. It seemed that she was allergic to everything. My family referred to her as a hypochondriac. My aunt was an interesting, eccentric woman.

Mom felt sorry for her sister, but she was sickened by her sister's inability to stand up for herself. Mom, on the other hand was strong, opinionated, and determined to make something of herself. Even though Mom was an obedient, compliant child who did everything she could to please her parents, it was to no avail. She never felt that she was ever "good enough." She was determined to be nothing like her mother—and certainly not like her sister. She loved and admired her older brother who tried to stand up to their overbearing dad.

Mom hated the gruffness of her dad and the way he berated her mother. She despised how he pitted her against her mother, criticizing everything his wife did, shouting hateful things at her. He insisted that my mom, at 12 or 13, make the meals, and then he would say to his wife, "She is a better cook than you. Why don't you cook like her—or iron, or sew, or clean the house like her?" The recollection of these memories used to make Mom cry, and she would get an angry faraway look in her blue eyes, clench her jaws, and say, "I hated him so much!" Then the subject would quickly change.

My mom shared the story of being struck so hard by her dad that she flew clear across the living room, hit the wall, and slid to the floor. She was in her teens and trying to become independent, but her dad had pushed her to the limit that day. She couldn't recall what had upset her so much, but she screamed at him, "You are just like Hitler!" This statement brought forth his fury, and he backhanded her. Her mother did nothing about it except to tell her that she needed to learn to shut up.

My mother said she was never allowed an opinion or to even think to challenge her dad on anything. When she did, rage was usually the outcome. How ironic then that while she may have hated his behavior, as generational curses so often happen, she would react in similar ways with her own children. I remember my mother's rage and anger vividly. And so, the curse kept cycling.

Once in a while Mom would go into detail about how her dad followed her to and from events and watched her like a hawk. The town in Colorado to which they had moved was a small, safe community, and she was never in any danger nor did she feel the need for protection. It confused her that her dad would be so "protective." Yet, more than confusion, it caused her to despise him. She wasn't allowed to go to the ice rink or roller-skating rink alone with her friends for fear that there might be a boy there. At most outings, she would be the only teenager with a parent attending. Her dad would "chaperone" her, and then sit there the entire time, watching her every move. She said this was so common that she didn't want to go out anymore. Friends always asked her why he was there, and she was so embarrassed by it. School functions and dances were the worst. She wanted to have a boyfriend and wanted the boys to like her, but she knew her dad would not allow it. Other than the school chaperones, he was the only parent to attend the school dances. He would just sit and watch. My mom said friends told her they thought it was "creepy." She agreed but couldn't get him to stop showing up.

Mom recalled how that, one day after school, she was a few minutes late arriving home after being with her friend Wanda, as her father waited for her at the door. She was sixteen years old and already "well developed," as she put it. After he screamed at her, he bent her over his lap, yanked her underwear down and began to spank her. She was mortified and traumatized by the event. I remember so vividly when my mom would tell me this story. She became distraught, with her hands shaking violently and tears running down her face in anger. She knew that he was jealous and controlling of her. "He treated me like I was his wife and not his daughter! I hated him for it!" she would vent, and then she would cry. "Why didn't Mom do anything? Why didn't she stand up to him? She knew what was going on!" she sobbed, and then there was silence.

After we would have these "heart to heart" talks, my mom would quickly pull herself together and move on to another topic. She was an expert at stuffing her pain. For some unknown reason, she confided in me. After my mother's death, some of these subjects came up during talks with my sisters, and they seemed shocked. I was shocked too, but it was that they didn't know. I don't know why my mom felt compelled to tell me. The only reason I could come up with was that, of all her children, I was the only one that attended church regularly. Oftentimes my mom and I would discuss religion. We talked about spirituality quite a bit. Many times we talked about forgiveness. She believed forgiveness was necessary, but she would clench her jaw and say, "I will never forgive my dad for what he did to me!"

When I was in my late twenties and early thirties, I spent countless hours visiting with my mom about life in general. These were the times during which she opened up to me in bits and pieces about her childhood. I pried her about her memories, and she always said that she had "blocked it all out" or that she didn't "want to talk about it; it's in the past." Now, years later, after having gone through my own traumatic self-discovery, I have my suspicions about the things my mother may have blocked out. I wish so badly she could have found peace and healing for what haunted her for so many years.

My mother was a shapely five-foot-two blonde who never went on a single date until she met that handsome man with the limp. It was 1949, and she was 20 years old. A girlfriend named Bertha Mae had invited her to a local community dance in the country. She was confident and self-assured as she visited with her friend and watched the people mill about. Music played and couples danced to loud guitar and fiddle tunes as she sipped punch near the refreshment table. Across the room, her eyes were caught by a tall, dark-haired "cowboy." Her friend knew the man he was talking with, and my mom asked about him. Without any hesitation, Bertha Mae introduced my mom to Benny, and Benny introduced her to the man who would become my dad. He was a 22-year-old rancher who lived ten miles outside of town. A conversation was struck, and, although my mom noticed my dad walked with a very pronounced limp, she didn't hesitate to accept the invitation to "shake a leg." They danced every dance for the remainder of the night. He began inviting her to other dances and social events and was essentially courting her. She was terrified to tell her parents that she had met someone, so she kept their dating a secret for quite a while.

Uncle Dale went off to be a "Seabee" with the Navy in 1950. My mom no longer had him to calm the waters at home when her dad erupted in angry tirades. Though she was 20 years old and held a full-time job as a secretary, she still resided at her parent's home. When she finally got up the courage to tell them she was dating someone, her dad waited on the front step as he brought her home so he could watch them. This prevented any good-night kisses. She exited the car and entered the house to receive the full interrogation about the date. She couldn't wait to get out of the house, but often felt sorry for my Aunt Mae who was still finishing up her senior year of high school. My dad was a likeable man and finally won Grandpa over. Their courtship lasted a little over a year, and they were married on July 25, 1951. My dad was 24, and my mom was 22.

My dad did not like my mother's name or the fact that it had been changed to a nickname. It was a male gender name, and he was uncomfortable calling her by it, so he simply didn't use her name. He only referred to her as "your mom" or "the wife." She would carry her masculine nickname all of her life, and it was carved on her headstone.

Stacks of photo albums sat on the old bookshelf in our home. When I was a kid, I would look through them for hours. I was fascinated by the black and white photos of me and my siblings when we were little. The later colored photos were more vivid and interesting to look at. The smiles on everyone's face and what seemed to be a loving, wholesome family used to make me feel good. But there was always a sense of sadness and almost disconnect. I would sit with my mom as she pointed out her favorite pictures. There was one of her in a one-piece bathing suit sitting beside a pool. She was pretty and had a beautiful figure. She would remind me, "I used to be thin and pretty, but that was before I had you twins." She would go on to say that she never could lose weight after having us. As a child, I took this to mean that it was my fault that she was heavier and not as pretty as she used to be. Whether she meant it to be hurtful or not, I internalized the comment and took it personally. She repeated those comments throughout the years as she looked at herself in the full-length mirror in the living room. "I used to be thin and pretty until I had you two. Now look at me!"

Through my years of education and my own journey of healing, I've discovered a great deal about family dynamics. The term "dysfunctional family" became very popular around the time I was in my master's program in the 1990s. I was teaching special education in Colorado, and the psychology coursework I took helped me to understand more of the issues I had to deal with. The home lives of some of the children I taught were disturbing. While some of my students had learning disabilities, many suffered with significant emotional problems that greatly hindered their ability to learn. Since then, I've come to understand more of the dysfunction that took place within the walls of my own home growing up.

The roles that each family member takes on within the home can shape the child from the moment they are born. There was a very sick role reversal between my mother and her dad that clearly damaged her as a young person. In my mother's case, she never realized that it had even taken place or that there was anything she could do about it. She just thought her dad was a mean, horrible man. She hated him so much, often repeating the words, "I will never forgive him for what he did to me!" She would never come right out and tell the deep, dark truth of what she went through as a child at the hands of her own father. She never sought help, and it never even occurred to her that she needed help for the repressed memories that she "blocked out." Otherwise, if she did recall what happened to her, she simply chose to never reveal to anyone the deep, dark secrets of her childhood. Her stern, staunch German heritage taught her to be strong. She didn't need anyone's help. She stuffed her emotions. I can only remember her crying on a few occasions. Each time it was during our "heart to heart" talks when I would prod her to talk to me. For some reason, I always felt my mom was hiding things. She was aloof and cold and very hardened when it came to talking about her younger life. I didn't even see her cry when my dad had his stroke or when her own mother passed away. Tears did not come easily for my mom.

My grandfather died in December 1964 of black lung from his years of chain smoking and his work in the coal mines. At the time, my twin sister and I were only six months old. I believe my mother fell into a terrible depression after the death of her dad. Though she was secretly glad that he had died, part of her truly loved him and longed to have a proper father-

> *The roles that each family member takes on within the home can shape the child from the moment they are born*

daughter relationship. Perhaps she longed for some kind of closure. Only God knows. She obviously had unresolved emotional issues.

In those days, it was rare to seek any kind of counseling for anything that might even hint of mental illness or depression. I don't believe my mother's problems really got bad until after she had had a few kids. The truth is that, until recently, I thought I had a fairly normal upbringing. I too must have been in some state of denial. My repressed memories also were buried in the deep recesses of my mind, and perhaps I too subconsciously thought that I would take them to my grave. If nothing else, I certainly minimized what I had gone through.

Looking back now, I can't help but wonder why I did this. Why so long after my mom's and dad's deaths did I start to see the truth of my childhood? Why am I a thousand miles away from any of my family? What role did my mother and dad play in shaping my life? Why am I the only child of this couple's six children to find refuge in a relationship with Jesus and a desire to find healing? Was my mom really the Christian she claimed to be? How do I reconcile all of the pain I endured at the hands of my own mother?

Unfortunately, my mother was not the only contributor to the painful upbringing I endured. There was a dad to consider as well. His name was Joe.

Chapter Notes and "Aha" Moments :

Chapter 4

Where I Came From: Dad's History

My dad's childhood was certainly no bed of roses. He was born the third child of a ranch family in Colorado. His grandparents were all immigrants of English and German descent. Upon entering the United States, the families moved from Virginia and the Carolinas, in the late 1880s, to homestead in Colorado. There was always a joke about my grandparents' union being like the divide of the Civil War. My grandfather's side of the family, which came from the North, always seemed to lord their superiority over my grandmother's family, who came from the South—they were more refined and sophisticated. It didn't help that my great, and great-great grandfathers were named Robert and Grant. It seemed a lifelong reminder of where they came from, and they were proud of it. So, the war of the North and the South raged on in a small ranch community in midwestern Colorado.

At two years of age, my dad became very sick and was taken to the hospital. His condition worsened, and he ended up at the Denver children's hospital where he was diagnosed with osteomyelitis. This is a bone infection caused by bacteria that enters the blood stream, either by an untreated wound or by an undetected break in a bone that hasn't healed. Despite treatment, the infection progressed, and he had to remain at the hospital until he was seven. During those five years, he only got to go home a few times. He hated going to hospitals for any reason and avoided hospitals at all costs. He said that he would get lightheaded at the smell of hospitals and was, therefore, not even present at the birth of any of his children.

The ranch where he lived when this happened with his mom, his dad, his ten-year-old sister, his eight-year-old brother, and his newborn baby brother was 125 miles from the hospital in Denver. His dad drove the only vehicle they had on an unpaved, dirt road to give blood transfusions to my dad at least twice a month. His poor little body was riddled with scars. His right arm, right shoulder, and right leg had to be scraped clear to the bone regularly to drain the infection out of his body. Through the course of this illness, he completely lost the hearing in his right ear. His right arm wasn't as strong as his left one, though he was right hand dominant, and his right leg didn't develop correctly, leaving it several inches shorter than his left leg and giving him a significant limp.

My dad loved his dad and shared with me how he would listen to every story his dad told him during the countless hours of visits to the hospital. I was amazed at his ability to remember some of the details. The Catholic nuns and nurses were his surrogate mothers. He may not have gotten the care from his own mother, but he certainly didn't go without attention, for the nurses pampered him, and he had fond memories of their care.

My dad showed me his precious toy "Blue Bird," a duplicate of the toy his dad brought to him at the hospital during one of his visits. It was a cast iron horse to put coins in. His brother got a red iron horse, but his was blue, hence the name "Blue Bird"—like the beautiful mountain bluebirds from home. He said he played with it most of the time, and it was his favorite toy. He even let some of the other kids play with it once in a while. Apparently, when it was time for him to leave the hospital, his beloved "Blue Bird" must have been mistakenly placed in the toybox by one of the nurses, and he didn't realize that it was gone until he was home. He seemed very sad when he told me the story, and I felt sorry for him. He was so fond of the gift that he searched until he found another one to replace it. He kept it on the top of his gun cabinet for years and told me he wanted my oldest son to have it when he was gone. It disappeared after his death, and I have no idea where it ended up.

My dad was very fond of his mother, a patient, loving, and gentle woman. I loved my grandma very much. She taught me to crochet and how to play solitaire. We played countless games of rummy too. She gave me buckets of empty wooden spools, and I built elaborate corrals and barns and pretended I was a rancher. I would round up my herds of cattle (usually rocks) and put them in my spool corrals. My sister used her buckets of spools as pretend dolls and girly things. I always wished I would have had a grandpa, but both my parents lost their dads before I could ever know either of them.

When Daddy was seven years old, he was finally released from the hospital in Denver. Only months after my dad's coming home, his dad had a massive stroke and died at the age of 42. My dad was devastated. To make matters worse, his older siblings commented to him that it was his fault that their dad had died. They told him that the stress, worry, and travel in having to take care of *him* wore him out and caused him to die so young. My dad lived with the guilt of this loss his entire life.

I remember him telling me that he blamed himself and felt that his siblings hated him for requiring so much of their dad. It seemed as if he just needed to vent, and I listened to him talk during our many hours of drive time checking cattle. I tried to reassure him that he couldn't have caused his dad's death. I told him that he was very blessed to have gotten to spend so much quality time with his dad before he died and that his siblings were probably just jealous that their dad loved him so much to have wanted to save his life by making that trip to Denver to see to it that he lived.

> *To make matters worse, his older siblings commented to him that it was his fault that their dad had died*

I harbored resentment toward my aunt and uncles for putting this kind of burden on my dad when he was just a boy. In those days, given his grave condition, it seemed as if his siblings preferred he would have died. The medical expense alone was a huge burden to the family, not to mention the fact that he was disabled. I always believed that my dad was special. I felt God had blessed him and allowed him to live for a purpose. He was a special man, and I loved him very much.

After the death of my grandfather, my great grandfather stepped in to help my grandmother, but that was short lived. My great grandfather had a massive heart attack within three months of my grandfather's death. So, my grandmother lost her husband and her dad within a three-month period and was left with four children to care for, one of whom was my dad, "the cripple," as he was called.

My grandmother's older brother Fred lived and worked together on the same ranch. He was my dad's uncle, and my dad had no use for him. Once my dad's dad (my grandfather) and my dad's grandfather had passed away, Uncle Fred basically took over the entire ranch and ran it for his own family's interest. My dad told stories of his cruel treatment and how that, even though my dad was somewhat limited and sickly, he was still expected to pull his weight with all of the chores around the ranch. At the same time, Uncle Fred's kids were spoiled, and he did not expect them to do nearly as much.

My dad told a story once that took place when he was around eight years old. He and his younger brother were given new ball caps. He was very proud of his and took good care of it. One day, my dad and his brother were out in the yard playing when Uncle Fred came riding up in the yard on horseback and began scolding the boys for some reason. Uncle Fred took down his lariat rope and roped my dad from horseback. The rope apparently knocked my dad's precious hat off, and it landed in the mud. My dad was so mad, he grabbed the rope and gave it a firm yank. Off came Fred, out of his saddle and into the big mud puddle. As my dad related the story to me, he laughed with such pride in having gotten revenge on his mean old uncle for messing up his new ball cap. He would have gotten quite a beating if Fred could have caught him, and, as he recalled, it would have been worth it.

My dad was a hard worker even as a child, and his disability didn't slow him down. He recounted stories of how he would run the bases at school and play all the normal games the other kids played. He was proud of the fact that he won perfect attendance certificates at school for not missing any days over several consecutive years. He went to school no matter how sick he was because he didn't want to be home with mean Uncle Fred. His uncle would send him to the field even when he had a fever, no matter how sick he was. He hated his uncle Fred and the way he treated everyone, including my dad's mother.

My grandmother remarried a well-respected man in the community just a year after the death of my grandpa. My dad was only eight years old, and this was difficult for him. Fred no longer had full control of the ranch, and that made my dad happy as he entered his teenage years. Yet, life was hard for my dad. His stepfather was a nice man, but he favored the Jehovah's Witness faith. My grandmother had a background in the Methodist Church, and, though she didn't attend church often, she did believe in God. She found herself at the mercy of her husband because she was a widow with four children and counted herself fortunate that a man would marry her with such a brood of kids. My dad remembered that, once Ray became his stepdad, there was never another birthday party, Christmas tree, or holiday celebrated as long as he was around.

Grandma and her new husband had one son from their marriage. My dad now had a half-brother, eight years his younger. My dad's oldest sibling was his sister who was eight years older than he was. She was sixteen when Grandpa died, and she had been very close to him. She did not approve of her new stepfather and wanted nothing to do with him. According to my dad, she made Ray's life miserable. He and my grandma divorced when their son was in his early teens. The older stepchildren bid Ray good riddance.

Because of the strict and odd beliefs of my dad's stepfather, my dad didn't have much use for organized religion. He believed in God but said that the great outdoors was his church and that he didn't need to go to a building to talk to God. Yet, he knew that the nurses and Catholic nuns prayed for him when he was so sick as a child. I told him I thought it was a miracle that he had lived and that I was glad he survived, or I wouldn't have been born.

I talked to my dad about God and about spiritual matters whenever the opportunity presented itself. He was happy to see the changes in me after I went through my horrible adolescent years. He knew that I attributed my change to the working of God in my life, and he didn't give me any grief about my new-found faith or about the fact that I attended church on Saturday. He thought it was peculiar, but, after I explained it to him from the Bible, he seemed to understand. He attended some of my son's school events and even respected the fact that I honored the Sabbath. I would not gather or brand cattle or do any ranch work on Friday evenings or Saturdays. My brothers weren't happy about the change, but my dad was the boss, and he made the decisions about matters on the ranch. Even my dietary differences were respected by my mother. I was ridiculed by my siblings, but it was only because they didn't understand. They considered me to be a "radical Bible thumper." I had grown up raising pigs, but, after 1984, I never ate another pork product of which I was aware. My conviction about eating biblically clean foods was pretty strong, and I made no exceptions.

Back to my mom and dad. They were married in 1951, and my dad's little herd of cattle grew on the land that they bought together not far from where he had grown up. Shortly after the birth of their first son, the milk cow kicked my dad during his morning chores, and the bone would not heal. He spent the next year in a cast with the doctors routinely draining the wound in hopes of saving the leg. He lost so much weight and became so weak that the doctor thought he would be better off if the leg were removed. It was amputated right below the knee. When he received his prosthesis, they made it the same length as his left leg and, suddenly, his limp was gone. My mom commented that he could finally dance better, though they rarely got the opportunity. His back and hips were better aligned, and the loss of his leg actually proved to be a blessing.

My dad was my hero. I admired him immensely and have many fond memories of him. He had a boot and saddle repair shop in town, though ranching was his passion. The pastureland that he inherited, leased, and was purchasing allowed him to establish his small cattle herd. My mother always said that she wanted to marry a "cowboy," yet I have vivid memories of her complaining that his cows were more important to him than anything. She was jealous of his cattle. I believe that caring for them was his way of escaping the reality of the home and the friction that took place there. He did not like the term "cowboy." My dad was a "cattleman" through and through. He left the term "cowboy" to the rodeo kids who strutted around like little bantam roosters.

When I was in kindergarten, my sister and I only went to school until noon, and Daddy picked us up most days. We would stay at his saddle shop until he went home or until Mom got off work and picked us up. Daddy would buy us bottles of soda pop, and, once in a while, we would go to the corner bakery to get donuts. We also went to Murphy's Poor Boy diner to get cheeseburgers on rare occasions, and sometimes my dad would splurge and get us chocolate milk shakes.

I loved to watch my dad work. He usually had his old radio tuned in to the local country music station, and he would sing along with Jim Reeves, Charlie Pride, and Hank Williams, Sr. He cussed on occasion when he accidentally hit his thumb with a hammer or stuck himself with a needle. I can still smell the leather, saddle soap, and rubber cement that he used to glue the soles of the boots on with. I loved the sound of the old sewing machine thumping and squeaking as it slowly stitched the leather pieces together in rhythmic bursts. I watched mesmerized as the needle picked up the thread, making neat rows across the beautiful pieces of leather that would soon be a pair of chaps, a rifle scabbard, or a holster for a pistol. With his rawhide mallet, he would strike the leather, stamping it as he tooled beautiful patterns into the leather. He also made custom bridles and repaired just about anything made out of leather.

I swept the floor and picked up after him as he worked. I was his little helper. He was a very tidy man, and everything had its place. He was a truly gifted leather worker, but my mother never appreciated him or his talent. She thought it was a waste of time and only a "hobby."

By the time I was entering the second grade, my mom insisted that he sell the shop and get a "real" job. She said that he wasn't providing enough for the family with his shop and part-time bus driving. I think it broke his heart, yet he still earned extra money working leather on the side at the shop at our home. Like his cattle, his shop was a way of escaping the chaos and moodiness of my mother. There was very little order in the house—just a lot of yelling and fighting.

My dad was not the typical man of the house. Mom wouldn't allow it. She was the disciplinarian and had the final say on most everything. My dad hadn't learned what a dad was because he hadn't seen fatherhood modeled for him. This was another odd family dynamic. His temperament was more like that of his mother's, and my mother acted like her dad.

In 1970, my dad went to work for the Fremont County Road Department while still maintaining his cattle herd. He had three sons and three daughters, and he wanted us to share his passion for ranching. Only a couple of us had any interest. I loved ranching and all animals, and I loved my dad.

My dad could do no wrong in my eyes, and, sadly, I excused his poor behavior. I pitied him and felt sorry for him and overlooked his abusive ways when he screamed and yelled and threw temper fits whenever things didn't go his way. Yet, he never laid a hand on me. I don't recall him giving me a single spanking. However, the harsh words that he used when I could not fulfill a particular demand, when I was a child, cut and scarred me deeply. I was made to feel stupid if I didn't know exactly which tool to hand him or if I couldn't run fast enough to head off a cow getting through the gate. He was quick to call me "stupid," "good-for-nothing," and other expletives that I cannot include here. However, my dad always had a way of saying that he was sorry without actually apologizing. After his emotional explosion, he would ruff up my hair or make some gesture that let me know that he still loved me. I don't know why, but I never felt a lack of love from my dad. I got affirmation from him. He complemented me when I sang silly little songs that I had learned at school. He thanked me when I did something for him. I always had a bond and a connection with my dad. I was so starved for love that I gobbled up any morsel of kindness I could get. I didn't receive that kind of affirmation from my mother and, consequently, I had very little connection to her.

I remember an incident that took place when I was about twelve years old. I had gotten off the bus as my dad was working in the yard. He greeted me, and I just kicked the rocks and headed off toward the reservoir near the corrals. I remember I was sitting there just crying, and I don't remember why, but, out of nowhere, there he was. He sat down next to me and asked me if I was okay. With his prosthesis, sitting like that was no easy feat for him. I remember pulling myself together and throwing a rock in the water and telling him that I had had a bad day. I'll never forget the impact his presence had on me. He had gone out of his way to notice that I looked sad, and he sought me out. I knew that he cared, and I always felt loved by my dad.

It is a sad thing to admit, but, as a child, I remember bargaining with God that He would let my mom die first. I couldn't bear the thought of losing my dad or the thought of being left alone with her.

When I think back about my parents and the dynamics of my family of origin, I can't help but wonder how different things could have been for my mother if she had only sought the help she needed for her traumatic childhood and her blocked memories. Oh how different things could have been if my dad could have sought help for his anger issues. He never dealt with the hatred that he had for his uncle Fred on top of the loss of his dad or the guilt that he felt over that loss. Both of my parents were abusive. They both had been abused. They had such limited tools in their parenting toolboxes, and I am one of the broken creations that they built. In my brokenness, I went on to build my own little broken people. Though these generational curses may weaken over the years, they don't go away, and my children were also damaged because of me. Yes, I carried on the generational curse. Thank God, I have sought help and healing!

Chapter Notes and "Aha" Moments :

Chapter 5

First Marriage

My mind drifted back to the time when I visited several different churches and found nothing that satisfied me. Most of my friends were still partying. In 1983, at nineteen years of age, I should have been off to college or making plans for the future. I still loved to ride horseback with my dad and round up cattle, brand, and do the other chores connected with a ranch. But I was confused and lost, and I desired the wholesomeness that I had started to learn in going to weekly AA meetings. I had no desire to find "love," and, after my previous abusive relationship, I was very distrustful of any man. I wanted to find a new love. Was Jesus, the Savior, the answer? Could I really get to know Him? Who was He anyway?

"Sit still! Keep your hands to yourself! Don't move!"

"Ouch!" I grimaced, as I shook myself back to reality and thought about the memories of sitting in the cold and sterile sanctuary of the St. Paul Lutheran church as a child. My mom squeezed my leg, and her nails dug into my skin. I was afraid to move. I sat dazed and terrified as the reverend droned on and frequently pounded the pulpit shouting hellfire and damnation to those who sinned and were "bad." I had heard repeatedly from my own mom what a "bad" little girl I was. I was convinced, at a very early age, that I was destined to burn in hell for everything I had ever done. God could only be harsh and mean, and I was going to pay for every wrong deed I ever committed. The words "God" and "love" made absolutely no sense to me. After going through the entire catechism class, memorizing countless scriptures and being confirmed at the age of thirteen, I still had not one clue about the love of God, Jesus, and the Holy Spirit, and I certainly had no knowledge of forgiveness, mercy, or grace. I saw only hypocrisy in religion, and I wanted no part of it. Yet, week after week, year after year, Mom would load us up in her blue 1970 Chevrolet Nomad station wagon, and off to church we would go.

Ah, then there were the catechism classes. A clear picture of my disregard for religion took place each Wednesday afternoon when I was in eighth grade. My friend Aubrey and I made our two-mile trek to the church by way of whatever alley we could take to avoid being seen while smoking our cigarettes. We would usually steal them from one of our friend's parents, or we had our older siblings buy them for us. I remember selling them to my friends for ten cents each. I was quite an entrepreneur. Anyway, my friend Aubrey and I would sneak through the alleys for several blocks until we came to the local 7-Eleven store on 9th street. We wandered through the candy aisle and took turns distracting the clerk while the other stuffed candy into her pockets. I became good at shoplifting, but I usually felt guilty about it, and that was as far as that bad habit went.

After our bouts of kleptomania, my friend and I would walk into the church basement at 4:00 p.m. and share our stolen candy with the other students in the catechism class. We even offered it to the reverend, who was happy to enjoy the treats with us. We opened our Bibles and study guides and proceeded with our lesson.

To this day, Aubrey and I reminisce about those bygone days and laugh at our stupidity. In somber tones, I think about the irony of it all and realize today, in my fifties, that I truly was a "bad" little girl. I was an even worse adolescent, and, while I did have a conscience and I knew what I was doing was wrong, I never understood how to have a relationship with Jesus. I had no knowledge of who He was. I'm sure my mother's intentions were good. She saw baby baptism and confirmation as a sure way of salvation for all six of us kids. She was just carrying on the Lutheran tradition.

Finally, in 1984, my drinking days were over, and I wanted a new life. I wanted to quit smoking too because I knew that cigarettes and drinking went hand in hand. It seemed wrong for me to ruin my lungs, and I was genuinely convicted that smoking was not good for me. A friend had recently given me a book entitled, "As Jesus Would Do." A new zealous Christian, I decided to put it to the test. I would gauge everything I did based on whether I could see Jesus doing it. I simply could not visualize Jesus with a cigarette sticking out of His mouth and smoke encircling His beautiful head.

One day while working at an electronics plant on an assembly line, I looked around and noticed some of my co-workers smoking. The small room was filled with a bluish haze of smoke, and I looked down at my ashtray full of squashed butts and ashes from my own cigarettes. It sat at the edge of my workstation where I was soldering wires together. I wanted desperately to stop this filthy habit, and I remember lowering my head and uttering a prayer. I didn't even really know how to pray. I simply talked to my new friend Jesus, and I'll never forget what happened next.

It's as if I can still see, feel, and smell the entire event as it happened. It was the first miracle I experienced when I decided to give my life over to Jesus and truly put faith into action. I challenged Jesus, and my prayer went like this: "Jesus, I don't want to smoke, but I crave these things so bad. If You want me to stop smoking, You will have to take the cravings away. I don't want to smell this smoke; it just makes me crave them more. Please help me. Amen."

I raised my head and looked around me. The scene was the same; the smoke was thick in the air, but, as I took a deep breath, I could not smell the smoke. I took a longer, deeper breath, and still, no smell. I remember feeling a sensation from the top of my head to the tip of my toes as my entire body erupted in goosebumps. I knew right then and there that Jesus had been present with me. He was letting me know that He would help me, that He was with me. I didn't stop smoking instantaneously, however. Yet, within two months, I watched Jesus take the craving from my body, and the desire to live healthier overcame the desire to smoke. I surrendered and gave it to God just as I had done with alcohol. He freed me from both addictions.

> *I knew right then and there that Jesus had been present with me. He was letting me know that He would help me, that He was with me*

I was so amazed by this miracle that I couldn't wait to tell my sister. As soon as work ended, I drove to where she worked and shared my story. She introduced me to a co-worker who had been witnessing to her, and I was invited to a Bible study group. I was eager to attend, as it gave me something to do in the evening. I hoped this would fill the hole that was left when I abandoned my friends, cigarettes, and alcohol. The Bible study was on Thursday evenings, and I went for several weeks before I was invited to join her for church.

I remember thinking how odd it was to go to church on Saturday. But then I remembered an incident from when I was just nine or ten years old. I was in the living room with my mom, and we were cleaning house. Her big Bible was sitting on the buffet table. I was dusting around it when I stopped to look at it. The Bible was open to the Ten Commandments.

I vividly recall reading them, and, when I came to the verse that says, "Remember the sabbath day to keep it holy," I turned to my mom, and asked, "Mom, what does 'sabbath' mean?"

"It's the day we go to church," was her response.

"But what does 'sabbath' mean?" I asked again.

"Go look it up," she said in a hurried tone.

So, I did. According to Webster, the Sabbath is "Saturday, the seventh day of the week, the day of rest."

"Why do we go to church on Sunday, Mom?"

With disgust and agitation, she told me to stop asking questions and get back to work! With my new-found knowledge, I closed the dictionary and carried on with my dusting, the seeds of that information lying dormant in my curious little brain until later.

Then, a few years later, a couple of the kids in my 4-H club roused my curiosity again regarding this strange day of worship. I loved my horse and couldn't wait to take him to the local county fair. "Jack" was my black, mixed breed "Heinz 57" horse. Not really much to look at, he was, to me, the most beautiful equine ever born. His stall was right next to the one used by the kids who were able to show their horses in the showmanship competition on Friday, who would ride in the equestrian classes on Sunday. But, Saturday, they were nowhere to be found. When I asked why they weren't there on Saturday, they responded that it was the Sabbath, and they wouldn't show their horse or do any work on that day. I remember thinking that that was surely *different,* but I didn't really pay much attention to it at the time. These seeds also were stored in the back of my mind for future reference.

So, when I was invited to attend church on Saturday with my new friends, those old memories surfaced, and I felt a conviction that there might just be something to this Sabbath day. I had finished a series of Bible studies on the topic and was convicted that Saturday was the day God intended for us to *"remember,"* but for some reason, the fact that I had had those previous experiences seemed to make the study even more convincing to me. Those early experiences were a sign from God Himself that He was preparing me for the meeting place at which I would finally learn the truth about Him.

I'll never forget being greeted by the sweetest little gray-haired lady when I entered the church that Sabbath morning. Her name was Eleanor, and she looked familiar. She asked if I remembered her.

"You look familiar," I said.

"I'm the lady that helped you when you got bit by that dog at your friend's house," she smiled.

"Oh, that's right! You're a nurse, and you put that wet washrag on my arm while I waited for Carla's mom to come get me." I grinned, almost in embarrassment.

"Yes, that's me," she smiled. "I'm also the nurse who brought you into this world," she said with a chuckle.

"What are you talking about?" I asked.

"I was the nurse that helped deliver you and your sister at the Colorado Hospital." Then she told me the story of my birth. "Oh, how I prayed for you little girls," she said, as she looked to the floor. "You were special little twins, and I worried about you."

Then she smiled, and I thanked her and headed through the doors to the worship service.

Wow! I thought to myself, as I entered the sanctuary that March morning. There sitting in a pew all by himself was my high school driver's education teacher. I really liked him, and he was one of my favorite teachers. He was kind and helpful and really took an interest in the students. He nodded at me with a smile, and I felt so at home in that church. I experienced God on a much deeper level in just those few short minutes than I could have experienced in weeks of studying by myself—or in the years that I had attended my mother's church as a child.

"I was the nurse that helped deliver you and your sister at the Colorado Hospital"

Later that day, I called my mom and told her about Eleanor. Mom remembered her and said she had some pictures of her holding my sister and me when we were just minutes old. She said that she would get them out of her photo album so I could show them to Eleanor the next time I saw her. I did, and Eleanor got a kick out of seeing those old photos. We would become very close over the next few years. She was a very special person to me.

While attending the Seventh-day Adventist church, I also met the man I would marry. We had a short courtship, as I considered myself a "born again virgin." We did not have premarital sex, and I was so happy to be finally on "the right track." After my baptism, I felt I had a new lease on life. By the time I was 21, I had my first son and was so happy to be a stay-at-home mom. Two years later I would have another son. Both of my sons were wanted, and planned pregnancies. I was worried that I wouldn't be able to have children. But that is a completely different miraculous story.

We purchased land near my family's ranch. I continued building the small herd of cattle that I kept with my dad's and brother's cattle. We all worked together on the family ranch. My husband was very citified, but he did try, and my family welcomed him and his attempts at learning to be a rancher. He resented the cattle, much like my mom resented my dad's cattle. I remember that, during one of his fits of frustration, he told me that it was either him or the cattle. After that emotional episode, he had a dozen roses delivered with a note of apology.

Our marriage seemed good, and I was fairly happy. But, once the boys began attending our local church school, I became bored. We didn't have health insurance, and I wanted to spend the summers with my sons. The logical solution was to apply at a public school. I was hired as a teacher's aide, and, within two years, I decided to continue my education to become a teacher. Life seemed complete. It was 1993.

My husband was a solid Christian man, eight years older than me, and dedicated to the church and his sons—but, most of all, dedicated to his job. A self-employed realtor, my husband provided well, though he was distant and not very capable of expressing or accepting emotions. I, on the other hand, prided myself on having good communication skills. Very expressive and wearing my emotions on my sleeve, I could light up a room with laughter and entertainment. Unfortunately, I could also be the cold bucket brigade with the perfectionistic, opinionated, and stern strictness that I inflicted on my innocent sons and husband. Apparently, my behaviors had been chipping away at our marriage for quite some time. However, because of my husband's lack of communication and my lack of understanding regarding my childhood dysfunction, I was oblivious to the marital erosion.

I learned early in life about how to maintain strict discipline—keeping a child in line simply by the raising of an eyebrow or the clearing of the throat. It makes a parent look good for having such *well-behaved children*. What I didn't realize until far too late was that I was terrifying to my children. Just as I had been terrified of my mother and how she "kept me in line" through her explosive but subtle anger, I too was keeping my sons in line. I don't recall spanking them past the age of four. All I had to do was look at them or start to count to three, and they didn't wait to find out what might come next. I always thought they *respected* my authority, but it was fear, just plain fear. It was the same fear I had had for my mom.

For a very long time, I have regretted using my passed-on disciplinary strategies. Though my children say they've forgiven me for being such a "dictator," I still have remorse over the damage I inflicted upon them.

More than the regret I have for being an overly strict and, therefore, abusive parent is the regret that I have for waiting so long to seek help for the sadness and sorrow that seemed to always hover over me. The pain that I inflicted was caused because I was in so much pain myself, though I didn't realize the source. The old adage, "Hurt people hurt people," was certainly true in my case.

Society only recently seems to have recognized that you don't have to physically beat a child to be an abusive parent. Emotional abuse is a cruel form of torture. I would rather have been beaten than to have suffered the abuse my mother inflicted. She ignored me, alienated me, and withheld her attention and affection as a form of discipline. This left me with deep, invisible scars of insecurity and of feelings of never being good enough. The silent treatment always left me wondering what I had done wrong.

After the death of my mother, I remember feeling so lost and alone with no one to go to. Did the loss of this enmeshed relationship with my mom cause my "God hole"? Was it I who was actually incapable of love? Did I not know how to love my husband? Had the conditional love my mother showed me been the only kind of love I understood? I sought help from my pastor; I had grief counseling. I even saw a marriage counselor for several months. My husband went to a couple of sessions but decided it was my issue, and he quit attending. Looking back now, I simply didn't know what questions to ask. I sought help, but no one knew how to help me.

I worked so hard in an attempt to get my mother's love and approval, and our relationship was tense. However, once I got married and had my two precious sons, she commented that I had finally "gotten my act together." At last, she was proud of me. We became very close. I'll never forget the loneliness I felt while just going through the motions of life without really living when she died. I felt numb. I recall my husband saying in October 1999, just three months after Mom's death, "It's been three months; you've had enough time to grieve; you need to get over it." His callous tone solidified just how little he really cared.

It was during an argument just a week later that he informed me that he hadn't loved me for about ten years and that he didn't want to be married to me anymore. I remember how the hollowness of losing my mother, now compounded by the reality of my husband's not loving me, gave me just the nudge to leave home. The following week I found an advertisement for a little mobile home in a nearby town, and I moved out. Our divorce was not final for another eighteen months, but we had no physical contact during that time. I poured myself into finishing my master's degree in special education, and I didn't have any time to consider seeing anyone, nor did I have the desire to do so.

There was a country song at the time by Tim McGraw entitled, "Angry All the Time." The words stuck in my mind and my heart broke as I listened to it. I truly did not know why I was angry all the time. There was just a hollow, black cloud that hung over me no matter what I did. I remember sitting in the pickup, crying because the song impacted me so deeply. My "God hole" was getting bigger and bigger when I thought it had been filled.

I had everything in the world I could possibly want. I had a financially supportive husband. I had two of the sweetest sons in the world, a wonderful church family, a beautiful home in the country, a good job as an educator—the list goes on and on. Yet, for no reason known to me, I seemed to be angry all the time. I prayed; I asked the pastor and friends to pray for me; I worked hard. I did everything I thought humanly possible to keep myself "happy." Yet still I had so much sorrow and sadness, guilt, shame, anger, anger, anger! And I had no idea why. I tried surrender. Though I no longer attended AA meetings, I was familiar with all twelve steps, and I knew that surrender was crucial to my healing. Yet, I didn't know what I needed to surrender. I still didn't have an answer for the anger problem.

We took turns sharing our 12 and 14-year-old boys. All three remained on my employee insurance. Then in 2001, my husband informed me that he was dating someone, and I was served with divorce papers. The marriage was over, and our divorce was finalized on September 14, 2001. Once again, the reality of "conditional love" hit me. I would come to realize that, while I wasn't the perfect wife and mother, there really was no grounds for my divorce, or that of the man I would come to marry. Our spouses simply made a choice to stop loving us.

The next five years, I attended church in neighboring towns because I didn't want to run into my ex and his new wife. I found out later that he wasn't attending. I decided to focus more on getting some of my songs recorded.

I took a trip to Tennessee and recorded a CD of my original songs. Within three months of getting the final product, it occurred to me that I had used my married last name on the CD jacket when I was taking my maiden name back. It was too late to change the labels. I clearly hadn't thought that through very well.

And then, in August 2002, I had a ruptured disc in my neck and needed immediate surgery to fuse two discs together. In the process of the next year, my vocal cords were strained, and I was unable to sing as I once had. My stamina was waning, and I found that singing more than four songs consecutively caused a raspy outcome. My swallowing was also affected, and, needless to say, my hopes and dreams of launching a music career were slipping further and further away. The problem may have been that it was *my* plan, not God's plan. So, I put singing on the back burner and let it just stew.

I accepted an offer to be the special education director at a youth correction facility that was just being built. My sons were now in high school and growing up. After my 20-year high school class reunion, I reconnected with a guy I dated way back then. It was a mistake to think that he had changed, but he did go to church with me some. His heart was not in it, however, and I really wanted a solid, Christian man in my life. That was another failed relationship.

I watched my horse graze in my two-acre backyard while I composed a list of criteria that the next man would have to live up to. I talked it over with God and decided that, if I were going to step out in faith, He would have to find me just the kind of man I wanted and needed. The list was long and complicated. It seemed to me that no man could possibly exist that would fit this unrealistic request. But he was out there, and I was about to be introduced to him. God is good!

Chapter Notes and "Aha" Moments :

_____

_____

_____

_____

_____

_____

_____

_____

_____

_____

_____

_____

_____

_____

_____

_____

Chapter 6

My Do Over

Not everyone has an opportunity to start over, but I am one of the fortunate people who got a second chance. I am living proof that God is merciful. He forgave my stupidity and heard me when I sought Him. I was ignorant of how far I had strayed from His path and oblivious to how much I needed to change. I discovered I wanted a *do over*.

My *new* story began in 2006 when I made the conscious decision to surrender everything to God. I had escaped the unhealthy relationship with my high school sweetheart in 2005. Once again, alone and lonely, I was determined to find a man to share my life with who was committed to God first and then to me. After all, God did not create us to be alone.

Because of a mutual acquaintance, I responded to an email from a man who had a similar background to mine. We were both born and raised on cattle ranches, and we were of the same faith. I was intrigued, and our emails quickly turned into phone calls, and, before long, we had agreed to meet in person. He was then residing in Alaska, so I flew up to meet him in March of 2007. It was an instant connection, and it almost seemed as if he were the missing piece to my puzzle. I wondered where he had been all my life. It seemed as if we had known each other forever. Leaving after getting to meet him in person was difficult, but we continued our lengthy phone conversations and emails.

I enjoyed the hours and hours of getting to know him, and I mused at the checklist I had made and how he was meeting my stringent requirements. He had left his ranch life after forty years to pursue a new calling, and, after going through a divorce himself, had decided that being alone was not what he wanted either. Our courtship seemed more of an interview process than dating. We both knew what we wanted in a mate, and we were honest in asking the right questions. We both watched for "red flags" and "deal breakers" and vowed that, if one of these came up, we would cut off the relationship. Nothing worthy of ending our courtship arose.

While Alaska seemed like a world away, I found myself genuinely falling in love with him. I've never prayed so fervently in my life. This was going to be a major life change for me, and I needed clarity and an "okay" from God, what I would later call my "God nod."

> We both watched for "red flags" and "deal breakers" and vowed that, if one of these came up, we would just cut off the relationship

His children were 11, 14, and 17, and he wasn't willing to uproot them. He shared custody with his ex-wife and spent as much time with them as he could. He tried to keep the relationship strong despite his ex-wife's distortion of the truth. Unfortunately, she tainted the kids minds with lies about him. This was difficult for me to understand, given my amicable divorce. My sons were already 18 and 20 years old and gaining more independence. In fact, my youngest son had just enlisted in the U.S. Marine Corps. My oldest son had purchased a home and was self-supportive. As far as I could see, my job as a parent was reaching its expiration date. I believed that my only role as a stepmother would be the occasional weekend. There is no "Stepparent" manual, and I thought this would be a role I could accept. As much as I loved my cattle and the beautiful state of Colorado, I felt a strong pull to the north. I took the opportunity to meet his extended family in his home state of Oregon, and he came to visit my dad and my sons in Colorado.

My prayer and study time kept taking me back to Abraham and the story of his leaving his homeland. I needed a change, and, with God's leading, I became willing to leave all I had ever known to marry this wonderful, godly man and move to Alaska. It was an answer to my prayer and a brand-new beginning for me. Unfortunately, even good changes can bring about stress and anxiety.

Exactly one month to the day after I left Colorado, my dad passed away suddenly. It was just two days before our wedding day. Nearly eighty years old, my dad had been confined to a wheelchair while still living in his own home. He had health care providers caring for him, and I had checked in on him from Alaska by phone every day. He still had his faculties, and, though he seemed sad that I had moved away, he was happy for me. I was grateful that he and my fiancé got to meet. I was very close to my dad, so the joy of my new marriage was overshadowed by his death. A bright spot in the wedding was that my sons came to Alaska to walk me down the aisle. My oldest son who recently broke his ankle, was wearing a walking cast from a recent 4-wheeling accident, and my younger son, wearing his gorgeous Marine Dress Blues, got to take a leave of duty. They seemed to like my new husband and were happy for me. It was a very memorable day. Instead of a honeymoon, we took a trip to Colorado to attend my dad's funeral. I was devastated but also at peace that he would be resting and no longer suffering.

Then, two weeks after my dad's death, I found out my son was being deployed to Iraq. I feared his joining the Marines, but I was so proud of him. All of the changes were apparently taking a toll on me. While I had so much joy in my new life, I had loss and grief. I was depressed and became sleep deprived. I saw a doctor, and he prescribed antidepressants to help get me through these life transitions.

Within a year of my dad's death, my emotional state had improved. My son, the Marine, was still alive and all seemed well. My husband had been contacted twice about going back into full-time ministry in the previous years, and he turned down both calls. But once again, a call came, and, after much prayer, he accepted it. Another change! I enjoyed the one year spent in Alaska and felt fortunate to have seen more of the state than many who have lived there a lifetime. My husband hauled fuel all over the state as well as all over the Yukon Territory in Canada. I was blessed to be able to go with him. It was an exciting adventure, to say the least. He knew he would miss seeing his kids, but visitations hadn't worked out as he had hoped they would. So, we headed to the lower forty-eight.

The transition of stepping into the role of a stepmother went well concerning his oldest child. The fact that my husband's oldest child was more mature was a factor, yet his being a son made it far easier. His daughters made it clear from the beginning that this was not going to be a smooth ride for me. They did not even show their dad love and affection because of the negative influence of their mom, and they had no intention of befriending some strange woman. The younger daughter cared more for her dad, so she made some effort. However, her love for her dad would prove to be a wedge in our marriage down the road. My issues with my mother and her apparent issues with her own mother became trigger points that kept us from forming a healthy mother-daughter relationship. I still hold out hope that there can be healing for all of us. I just know that divorce is devastating to everyone involved.

Now, in getting settled into a new home, with a new job and a new church, life was good. With my husband a pastor, life had a new set of challenges. Yet, all in all, I seemed happy. The next five years were spent learning what being a pastor's wife is all about. I loved the fact that I spent more time in my Bible. My relationship with God was growing, and I felt true contentment for the first time in my life. I also had the privilege of serving as the Shepherdess President for nearly five years in our conference.

Of course, the devil hates it when people have new, revived energy to put toward God's work. He had a brand-new target—*me*. I was beginning my third year of teaching special education in the public-school system when I began having health problems again. It was 2012. Old familiar pain returned, and another disc ruptured in my neck, sending me back for my second surgery. I now had discs five through seven fused. I chose to quit my teaching job.

This proved to be a blessing because I could now go with my husband to visit church members. I was also able to attend every funeral and engage in music ministry at local nursing homes on a regular basis as I had done in Colorado. I loved this new freedom, though I had no income. I was able to teach as a substitute, which allowed for flexibility, and I did earn a small amount of money.

In 2013, the opportunity came up for a full-time elementary P.E. (physical education) position. Hoping to put away some extra money, I applied for the job and began teaching in the fall. It would certainly be a change from teaching special education, but I thought I'd try it.

One of the kindergarten students in my P.E. class was a cute little five-year-old girl with messy blonde hair and a severe learning disability. Her behavior was good aside from the occasional refusal to follow directions. She would throw herself to the floor and cry. I would simply remove her to a safe place to sit, and she would quickly rejoin the group activity.

Once in a while I would hear her screaming in the halls. I'd look out from the gym and watch her writhe and swing her little fists in fits of anger as she lashed out at the teacher's aide who was assigned to work with her. She had a terrified, faraway look in her eyes, and it would send chills up my spine. When I inquired about her behaviors, I was told that she had been placed in foster care after being permanently removed from an abusive home life in which she had been tortured and sexually abused from the time she was an infant.

In all the years I had taught special education and dealt with children who had emotional disabilities, I had never been affected like this.

Apparently, the awareness of this little girl's situation and seeing the behaviors in her must have triggered something in me. Blocked traumas of my own infancy and childhood began to emerge.

I began having short flashbacks and fragmented memories of abuses that had happened to me in my childhood. I woke up in the middle of the night shaking so violently that I woke my husband up. We would go to the couch, and he would hold me and wipe my forehead as I would sweat and cry and wail. The anxiety got worse, and I got to the point that I didn't want to go to work. I loved my job and the kids, but I couldn't control the outbreaks of anxiety, which came out of nowhere. There were many occasions in which I was terrified and thought I was going to die. Other times, I welcomed the idea of death and wished there could be an end to the suffering. I confided in a church member who was a physician's assistant, and she referred me to a doctor. Once again, I was put back on an antidepressant and another sleep aid. Because of the changes I had gone through in the last several years and the stresses of it all, it seemed to so consume me to the point that I needed to seek help from more than just God. I recognized my need of God most of all, but I also realized I needed guidance from a professional to help get some clarity and perspective on what I was dealing with.

I began questioning whether I should have taken this new job, though I did manage to finish out the school year. I signed my contract for the following year, hoping that the summer break, some rest, and not being around the students would bring about needed healing. I could start fresh in the fall. However, within a month, the anxiety returned. By November, I was having daily panic attacks. I missed the flexibility of being a substitute teacher, and I decided to resign. Now, I could sub if I felt up to it and focus more on healing. I needed to get to the bottom of these haunting flashbacks.

Chapter Notes and "Aha" Moments :

_____

_____

_____

_____

_____

_____

_____

_____

_____

_____

_____

_____

_____

_____

Chapter 7

What is EMDR?

Maybe God allowed me to accept the P.E. teaching job so I could have my trauma revealed to me. Perhaps it was His intention to use it as a catalyst to bring me healing. Of all the years of teaching students with emotional issues, it's ironic that a child in my P.E. class would set it all in motion. Looking back, I wink at God for the plans and miracles He's been working out for me along the way.

As a special education teacher, it seemed as if I did more "counseling" with my adolescent students than teaching. I just did it without the title or degree of "counselor." Many of my students' academic failures were a direct result of their emotional baggage and lack of self-esteem. The abuses I read about in their files were disturbing, and that's why I'm shocked that none of it caused the reaction that I had from little Leah.

Of course, being in the public-school system, I was never able to give any spiritual advice (though they certainly could have used it). Yet, I was able to give them a sense of belonging, and I tried my best to boost their confidence in themselves. I wanted students to focus on their success and not their failures, their ability and not their disability. I *counseled* and listened as I taught, and I prayed for them on my own time. I found teaching quite gratifying. I always tried to empower my students, and I taught them to be resilient. In hindsight, I couldn't help wondering if I was drawn to work with these types of children because of my own hidden emotional trauma. I obviously had an empathetic bent toward them, and I've always secretly desired to be a counselor in some capacity. Perhaps as a special education teacher I was too close to the situations to see my own need.

In my time of unemployment and during summer breaks, I had done coursework through AACC (American Association of Christian

Counselors). The AACC coursework has proven to be a helpful tool. Generally speaking, just being a good listener is a ministry in itself, and I feel blessed to help my husband. In the future, I'd like to enroll in more classes so that I can become a licensed counselor if that is the path God leads me toward.

Being a pastor's wife also gives me opportunities to "counsel" hurting parishioners. In many cases, the topics that women bring might not be appropriate for my husband to discuss with them, and he never visits women alone anyway. Because of my background, I've been able to share my testimony. Being a recovering alcoholic and having gone through a divorce, I believe I have a great deal of experiential advice to offer. But more importantly, in listening to their stories, I can empathize and offer suggestions and possible strategies. I always give the disclaimer that I am not a licensed counselor or therapist, and, when necessary, I refer them to professionals when the situation is beyond my expertise.

> *The real issue became apparent that, while I'm helping to fill other's "God hole," my own "God hole" was getting bigger and bigger*

I'd like to believe that, as a pastor's wife, I've been fairly successful at helping people. Yet, because of my own recent pain, my secret life and the image of having it all together were going to be exposed if I didn't get help for myself. The real issue became apparent that, while I'm helping to fill other's "God hole," my own "God hole" was getting bigger and bigger. It is difficult for wives of pastors to risk reaching out to people, for even those they feel they can trust. We try to be transparent but cautious. We try to be as "human" as possible while maintaining a certain amount of "holiness." I'm not sure people realize the perceived expectations placed upon the wives of pastors. It is no easy job, and I was being emotionally drained.

Then it suddenly occurred to me, as I thought to myself, *When and where am I getting my help from?* Bookshelves are lined with self-help techniques. Libraries overflow with "how to" literature that gives ideas and suggestions. My head spins as I finger through the books that will "cure" me. Yet, I don't purchase them. I go to God; I read my Bible; I pray for a miracle. It's not that I was in denial about needing help. It just seemed ironic to me that, for the last twenty years, I had been in the position of helping others, and now I had to recognize my own need. *I feel empty. I feel hollow. I had been running on empty, and now I was out of gas.* The sudden changes in my life over the past few years had finally come to a head.

For many years, I have referred to what I call my "God hole." I've alluded to it in previous paragraphs. I firmly believe every human has this hole, this void. Since the fall of humankind and the entrance of sin, we humans, who were originally created to be perfect and sinless, now possess a natural, fallen nature. Sin has caused a separation from God. But I believe that we still—perhaps *unknowingly or subconsciously*—have a desire to be loved by and to love the One who created us to be perfect. I believe we all long for this wholeness with our Creator. When we are going through trials and sin creeps in and gets a grip on us, we become desperate. We grasp at anything to make us feel better. We try to fill our "God hole" with stuff to satisfy the longing that we all possess. This void, or "God hole," can be satisfied with but one thing—God.

I've discovered that my "God hole" first appeared when I was a child. Many people suffer what I did. Damage done to us may seem small or insignificant because we didn't understand that what others did to us was wrong. We took the blame for the "bad" that was done to us. Essentially nothing was resolved; the pain lay dormant; healing didn't take place, and the hole grew. As we age and mature, the pain continues to grow—as does the "God hole." Ultimately our desire to fill this "God hole" causes many of us to self-medicate. Instead of turning to God, we turn to the world and its addictions—alcohol, tobacco, gambling, food, sex, whatever happens to be our "drug of choice." These addictions can be fully surrendered to God. He will fill our emptiness if we seek Him and then let Him in.

I simply needed to find out what else was causing the anxiety and my overwhelming sadness. For years I had been helping others by listening and empathizing with their needs, yet I hadn't had anyone other than my husband to share my issues with, and I began to feel very depleted. I no longer felt the need of AA meetings and did not attend. I have learned since that many pastor's wives suffer a loneliness that is unique to this profession.

I knew I needed to get professional help, and I discussed it with my husband. I remembered the therapist I used to visit years before. It was after the death of my mother when I was going through my divorce in 2001 that I sought him out. He attended my church while living in Colorado and specialized in the therapy of EMDR (Eye Movement Desensitization Reprocessing). I found this form of cognitive psychotherapy to be the most helpful in dealing with the crises I was experiencing at the time.

At first, I was apprehensive and concerned that EMDR might be some form of hypnosis or new age meditation like I had experienced during my stay at an alcohol treatment facility when I was eighteen. However, I quickly discovered that it was exactly the kind of treatment I needed.

I contacted Ron, my therapist in Colorado, and we attempted a few therapy sessions using Skype. Unfortunately, the long distance and time delays on the computer made it impossible to continue the treatments in this manner. My husband and I decided to go to Colorado and spend two weeks doing intensive EMDR therapy sessions. The appointments were set up for daily visits, and we were on our way. There was an amazing amount of healing that took place, but future treatments were cost prohibitive because of the expenses of travel and accommodations. My progress was significant, but more traumatic flashbacks occurred. Two months later, I went back to Colorado for another ten days of intensive therapy treatments. I was placed back on an antidepressant to get stabilized.

The medication was helpful, as well as the strategies that Ron taught me to use. However, I needed to find a local EMDR therapist. I suspected that there were even deeper hidden issues that needed to be brought to the surface in order for me to find complete healing. I prayed and did an extensive google search and located a therapist within driving distance.

Our initial meeting proved to be successful, and I scheduled a follow up appointment. Getting to know more about me, she reached the same diagnosis as had my therapist in Colorado. My fears were recognized when horrific childhood trauma began to surface during EMDR sessions, and I was diagnosed with PTSD (Post Traumatic Stress Disorder) with complex trauma.

At this point in my story, I feel it important to explain the process of EMDR therapy. EMDR was discovered in the late eighties by Francine Shapiro, PhD. It has proven to be a successful therapy for the military when dealing with traumatized war veterans who struggle with PTSD. It is far more complicated than what I can explain in a few short sentences, but I will give a summarization of my understanding of how it works. I recommend going to these websites: www.emdr.com and http://www.emdr.com/frequent-questions/, if you are interested. There are many books available on the subject. My go-to book has been *Getting Past Your Past* by Dr. Francine Shapiro. I also gleaned a great deal of healing from Sandra L. Paulsen, PhD, who wrote, *When There Are No Words: Repairing Early Trauma and Neglect from the Attachment Period with EMDR Therapy.*

During a therapy session, the initial conversation between the patient and therapist takes place, and rapport is established. The therapist, by this time, knows something of the person's issues and is able to find a starting point for therapy. The therapist will attempt to bring up a "trigger," or a topic that will no doubt cause a reaction from the patient, and a traumatic event will come to the surface. The therapist will ask how disturbing the event is on a scale of 0 to 10. The therapist will either ask the patient to follow the therapist's finger with his or her eyes, moving back and forth, or the therapist will use a machine with a blue light that moves back and forth in a horizontal side-to-side movement. This is also known as bilateral stimulation. The therapist asks the patient to follow the blue light with his or her eyes while the discussion is taking place.

Other methods, which are just as effective and which I personally prefer, are the tapping method and the pulsating handheld tool, which sends a vibration from one hand to the other as the patient holds it. Whichever method is used, the primary intent is to engage the brain from left to right repeatedly. The rapid repeated back and forth movement of the eye or of the hand stimulates the memory of the trauma, bringing to mind things that have been repressed or blocked in the subconscious part of the mind. As the therapist asks, "What is coming up now?" it is as if the patient re-lives the event. Memories of every detail, which were perhaps stuck or locked away in the memory, come to the surface. Once a traumatic event has been brought to the surface and the brain is made aware of the old belief system, the thoughts, the trauma, and, most importantly, the lies, can then be desensitized. Each and every detail of the trauma does not have to be discussed or brought up. Once the general negative cognition is realized, the goal is to reframe it according to the positive cognition. An example would be: if I feel afraid, the goal is to reach a point where I feel safe.

> *The rapid repeated back and forth movement of the eye or of the hand stimulates the memory of the trauma, bringing to mind things that have been repressed or blocked in the subconscious part of the mind*

The therapist is highly trained in asking the right questions that will initiate a response from the patient and allow the traumatized person to see the truth as presented in the current situation. Once the reality of the truth is firmly reprocessed and reframed in the brain, it is locked in place, and the trauma begins to lose its affect because the new truth replaces the distorted beliefs once held. The strongholds of the lies are replaced with the truth and healing takes place. The therapist will then ask how disturbing the event is on a scale of 0 to 10 and, if the answer is a 2, 1, or 0, the trauma has been sufficiently dealt with and resolved. If the number is much higher, it is an indicator that there is still something hidden that needs to come out. The process is then repeated to re-visit the underlying issue.

It isn't as if the patient can ever forget the trauma. The memories of what took place are still in the mind, but the value of realizing and re-living the experience is that it allows the patient to see the event from an updated state of mind. The reality and truth are brought to the patient's awareness, and he or she no longer sees the overwhelming trauma as he or she did when the incident took place. It is re-processed in the current moment. The trauma loses its effect. It is as if the traumas that were stored in the darkest recesses, the little nooks and crannies of the mind come forward. Hidden no longer, they lose their power to cause the patient to be afraid, particularly when the traumas occurred, as in my case, when the person was a little child. As I now look up, in my fifties, at the monster, I find that it is no longer glaring over me. Living in the here and now, in my present state of mind, I re-live a portion of my life that I had no idea existed. The pain leaves as my therapist talks me through it, and I can honestly think about the event without it bothering me as it did just thirty minutes before the therapy session.

There is no hypnotism, and, at no time, is the patient unconscious or unaware of what is going on. There have been times that I have had to slow down or even come to a stop in therapy because there was a risk of my becoming re-traumatized. The therapist must be able to identify just how far a person can go in re-living the trauma.

At one time, it was believed that the neurons in our brains die once damage has occurred. More recently it has been discovered that damaged neurons can be healed. They can be "recharged" or regenerated, and this, in itself, is a medical miracle discovery. It gives greater hope to those who are suffering with mental illness. In recent years, the term "mental illness" seems to have lost some of its negative stigma. Those of us who were terrified to admit that we might have something wrong with us now feel empowered and willing to come forward. I've discovered through this therapy a new world of freedom, and I am eager and excited to bring it to the world's awareness.

EMDR is exhausting, but it is nothing short of a miracle. After each session, it can sometimes take an hour or two to decompress from the mental exhaustion that I have gone through. The discovery of this treatment has saved my life, and I know without a doubt that God helped me find out about it. I believe it is the key to my healing process.

Francine Shapiro, who discovered EMDR was one of my heroes. Sadly, she passed away June 16, 2019. She went to great lengths to see that EMDR is administered by only highly trained, accredited practitioners. Therapists must be approved and credentialed to follow her standard of protocols. She set up an ethics committee and an EMDR professional network. And, in 2013 EMDR therapy was approved by the World Health Organization (WHO) for use in treating PTSD, trauma, and other mental health disorders. I personally caution everyone to make sure you have a reputable, licensed therapist. There are no doubt some who would cut corners or try to duplicate this form of therapy and when done incorrectly, could cause harm and/or re-traumatize someone. Just a word of caution to the reader who wants to seek this amazingly successful form of therapy.

I'm off to my therapy sessions.

Chapter Notes and "Aha" Moments :

Chapter 8

Am I Loveable?

In my state of insecurity, my mind flooded with apprehension over who might have seen me pull into the parking lot. *Who may have seen me walk in? Who might be working at the office that knows someone I know?* I shook off the feelings, comforting myself with the thought that, in this day and age, there should be no shame in having to seek help. After all, I encountered people each week who were struggling in their marriages, with addictions, in financial crisis, or grieving over the loss of a loved one. A multitude of heartaches were a routine conversation for me, and I frequently suggested that these people seek professional help. Why should I be any different?

I felt like a hypocrite entertaining the slightest thought of shame and embarrassment over whether someone had seen me. While there has been an improvement, the reality and negative stigma for seeking help for depression or any form of mental illness is unfortunately alive and well, and I felt a twinge of it. For a split second, I felt inadequate. Who was I trying to kid—wanting to counsel students or thinking that I, of all people, could use my passion and empathy to help those in our church—when I myself need help? The cruel, niggling voice within my head rang out: *Who do you think you are?*

I'm proud of myself for doing something, I suddenly countered back. *I can't let the devil try to discourage me. He'd love it if I just stayed miserable, but I know, God, that You're going to help me.* My silent conversation complete, I settled into the waiting room chair I had selected.

Questions and trepidation arose as I looked down at my journal. At my last session, I was given the assignment of writing down all of the "rules" I was raised with from my earliest recollections. I was to document my life as a child and to detail my childhood "norms." What if I forgot something? I reviewed the list and thought how ridiculous they seemed to me, yet how real and solidly engrained into my belief system they were.

As I read them through, I could hear my mom's voice and see the sternness in my mother's countenance—the ice blue eyes glaring at me as she barked the words, the rules, the norms. "Sit still and shut up, children should be seen and not heard." "Get out of the way, you are always in the way." "You should be ashamed of yourself!" "Shut up that crying or I'll give you something to cry about." "You are so ugly when you cry, here look at yourself! See how ugly you are?" I blinked and then shuttered as I recalled my mother grabbing me by the back of the head and slamming the hand-held mirror toward my face, forcing me to look at myself while I was crying. "You are so ugly, look how ugly you are, Marie Ann!"

> *Why do these comments, which were made to "little Marie" forty some years ago, cause me so much grief today?*

Slapping the journal shut, I shook myself back into the present. I had only made it partway through the long list of "rules." There were so many more that I had listed. As painful as it was to have written them down the first time, I now realized how much greater angst it caused me to have to read them again. They were my reality. It was a way of life for me as a child. It only solidified in my mind just how horrible it made me feel now as an adult. Oh, how traumatic it must have been for me as a child. My heart went out to the little blonde kindergartener Leah that I used to teach. I wonder whatever happened to her and where she is today.

How am I going to make it through this therapy session? I thought to myself. *Why do these comments, which were made to "little Marie" forty some years ago, cause me so much grief today? Why do I have to face these demons now? Why can't I just ignore "it"? And what is the "it" I am trying to ignore?* I suddenly began justifying my childhood, and I heard my mother's words again: "No matter how bad things are, someone else has it much worse off than you do, so stop your belly-aching!" I began to feel for a moment that I shouldn't be seeking help. After all, I was fed; I had a home; my childhood wasn't as bad as others. It wasn't *that* bad. Then, as if an audible voice came out of nowhere, I heard, *Stop it! Stop justifying it!* and I realized that I needed to continue my quest for healing. I needed to stop denying the truth of my past.

"Come on back, Marie," I heard my therapist call.

I sensed this would be an intense therapy session, and it was. I was both exhausted and exhilarated as I left the office with a sense of peace and a pep in my step.

"Honey, I'm home!" I announced as I entered our cozy little home.

It had been a long but relaxing drive home, and I looked forward to wrapping my arms around my big, tall, loveable husband of nine years. It was now 2016. He is the most caring, concerned, godly man I've ever known. I praise God for him every day.

"How did today go?" He asked, as he grabbed me up in his arms and cradled me to his chest.

"It was very good—painful—but very good," I responded.

We went to the couch and spent the next hour discussing the events of the day. I shared with him what I had discovered during today's session, and he listened intently as he always did. He was used to me sharing my therapy sessions with him, and he genuinely wanted to know more. I appreciated that he never judged me or seemed disappointed in me as I shared more of what I had uncovered about my life prior to knowing him.

Once in a while, as I shared, he would put on his pastor's hat and begin advising and counseling me. I had to remind him that he was my husband and not my pastor, though oftentimes I felt I needed a pastor to share some of this with. What a dilemma I found myself in—living the role of a pastor's wife, while in need of a pastor, though not wanting my pastor to be my husband or my husband to be my pastor. I chuckled out loud as I shared with him, "What would I do without you, *my pastor?*"

He grinned, "Am I doing it again? Am I preaching to you?"

"Not too much. Just love me and listen to me," I said. "I don't expect you to fix me. I just want to be able to share what I'm learning. What I really need from you is prayer. I need you to pray that I will get the healing I need each time I go to therapy.

"You know I do, Honey," he said, as he looked lovingly at me and clasped my hands in his. "You are healing, you know? You've come a long way in the last few years and—don't forget—God knows what you need more than anyone else."

I squeezed his big hand and leaned over and kissed his cheek.

"I've got some things I need to do before supper," I said. "Thank you for listening and for loving me! I love you very much."

With that, I went to the den downstairs where I plopped down in the recliner and drifted off in thought. I began reflecting on the stories I had heard as a child about my birth—rather, about *our* birth. God's divine plan had been to give my parents a set of twins. Yes, I was the firstborn, and then, seventeen minutes later, the doctor engaged in the exhausting task of delivering my twin sister with forceps.

The story I heard directly from the mouth of the nurse, Eleanor, who assisted in our delivery, was that, when my mother drove herself to the hospital, they got her all prepped and ready and then, after I was born, the doctor asked Eleanor for another basket. My mother, weak and worn out from giving birth to me, asked, "What do you need another basket for?" and the doctor replied, "For this other baby you're having."

The story goes on that my mother then said, "I can't have another baby. Don't tell my husband; he will kill me." Eleanor said that the doctor was in as much shock as my mother, as this was the first set of twins he had ever delivered, causing things to be chaotic for a while. Eleanor thought it was funny that my mother said, "I can't have two babies!" She wondered how my mom planned on hiding the second baby from my dad.

My mom had shared this same story with us as we grew up, and she and my dad laughed a lot about it. My dad had been at a ranch rodeo roping event the day we were born, and, when he arrived at the hospital with the other siblings, they were all shocked at the news of twin girls.

My heart felt sad as I thought of my twin sister and how we hadn't spoken for the last sixteen years. After the death of my mother, it seemed that life for her changed. Indeed, life changed for the entire family, but, for my twin sister and the youngest of the three brothers, the change seemed to have been more traumatic. I was devastated too, and we all dealt with her death in different ways—some of us in healthier ways than others.

I'll never forget the day my sister called me and began screaming at me about how I had stolen her identity. She ranted and raved and used the most vulgar language until I finally hung up on her. I knew she wasn't doing well, and I simply didn't need to deal with her issues on top of my own, so I deliberately distanced myself from her. I began to distance myself from my entire family. The truth is, this was the beginning of my search for my own identity. I began to try to find out who I really was from this time on.

I heard my husband upstairs as I drifted back into the present day. I smiled at the thought of how blessed I was to have him for a husband. I couldn't help but wonder what affect my trauma and recovery was having on this precious man.

Would he have married me if he'd known what an emotional mess I would become? Did he have regrets and wish he could have found a wife who was healthier and had less baggage from her past? I quickly dismissed the thoughts, realizing that everyone has damage to some degree. After all, he wasn't perfect either.

My husband, like myself, had gone through a divorce years before. In both of our cases, our spouses were the initiator of the divorce, claiming that they no longer wanted to be married, that they no longer loved the one they had vowed "to love, honor, and cherish till death do you part." But I still recognized that my new husband had at least been raised in a far more wholesome Christian home than what I had known. He had a good foundation and had never left his first love—God.

Shortly after we were engaged, I had the opportunity to get to know his parents. I was amazed at the loving relationship they had, and I marveled at their profession of Jesus in every aspect of their lives. This seemed so foreign to me, yet I appreciated it and craved that kind of marriage for myself. I was determined to be the best wife I could be to this wonderful man, despite the less than loving home I had been raised in.

Our wedding took place in Fairbanks, Alaska, on a sunny July evening. We had decided that, with our brand-new marriage commitment, we also wanted to make a fresh start with God. We were both re-baptized in the Chena River just hours before the wedding. It was a beautiful way to begin our life together. Four of our five children were present. My husband's youngest daughter, eleven years of age at the time, chose to go to summer camp instead of attending our wedding. I was hurt by this and felt that she should have been there. But she wasn't. Today, after nearly thirteen years of marriage, all five of our children have yet to be in the same place at the same time.

So far, our marriage had been very good, though not without the typical stresses. Yet, I felt I had truly found love at last. But did I truly love him? Was I capable of love?

Am I a good wife? I sat up alarmed, as if I had been shocked into reality. The sudden thought that I had not truly been loved by my own mother made me question my own ability to love. This horrible lie that I had believed for nearly fifty years all came back to me now, and I felt a twinge of anxiety building up in my body.

What a failure I am! I thought to myself. I gave up on a marriage of fifteen years, walking away because I didn't feel loved or appreciated. *I absolutely need to understand what love is so that history does not repeat itself!* "Oh Jesus," I prayed, "help me to understand love. Teach me Your love. Am I loveable?"

Chapter Notes and "Aha" Moments :

_____

_____

_____

_____

_____

_____

_____

_____

_____

_____

_____

_____

_____

_____

_____

_____

Chapter 9

Conditional Love

Sitting alone in my downstairs den, I thought of a saying I had once heard: "Yesterday is history. Tomorrow is a mystery. Today is a gift from God, and that's why they call it the *present*."

Oh, how I would love to just live in the present and move forward," I thought to myself. *Yet, the past still keeps haunting me and, while I am healing with each EMDR session, there is still so much trauma left to discover. Can I really get to the root of my feelings of unworthiness and self-loathing? Can I ever really stop being angry?*

I looked across the room at my desk that sat in the den. It was covered with papers when I normally had a very neat desk. That day it looked messy and disheveled. *What a slob!* I thought to myself. And, out of nowhere, I was reminded of another childhood incident, another memory of my mother's conditional love.

"Is my mom there?" The timid voice asked, as I spoke into the black rotary phone that hung on the paneled wall of the old ranch home. I waited for the voice of my mother to answer.

"What do you want?" she said, with a tone of hurried sternness.

"I wondered if you could bring me home a candy bar tonight," I suggested timidly.

"I suppose," she responded. "Have you done all the chores on the list?"

"Yes, the house looks good," I proudly announced.

> *I could nearly taste the goodness of this newly invented candy bar. It was in the early 1970s, and I was eight years old*

"We'll see. What kind of candy bar do you want?"

"A Hershey Special dark chocolate."

I could nearly taste the goodness of this newly invented candy bar. It was in the early 1970s, and I was eight years old.

Our typical chores consisted of feeding and watering the rabbits as soon as I got off the bus around 4:00 p.m. Then, one of us would feed the dogs and cats and head to the house to start the indoor chores. There was always a list on the kitchen table that Mom had left. Years later, when questioned why we had so many chores to do, Mom would jokingly say that it was her way of keeping us busy and out of trouble. I suppose there is some valid reasoning there, but I felt like a slave, nonetheless. The list consisted of vacuuming the house, dusting everything, gathering all the dirty clothes and making sure that they were in the laundry baskets. Likewise, the coal bucket had to be emptied of its ashes and filled back up with coal. The wood box had to be filled to the brim. She expected an overall tidying up of the house, which didn't seem like too much to ask, and, though I probably had homework to do, the chores were the priority.

I relate this from my perspective even though my twin sister was there too. She, however, would usually go directly upstairs to play with her Barbie dolls the minute we got finished with the "chores." All I knew was that Mom, like her dad, ruled the roost with an iron fist, and I wanted to keep her happy.

I cannot speak for my sister's perception of what took place in that old two-story home on the Phantom Canyon Road. This is simply how I remember my life as a "latch-key" kid. I was always eager to get the work done so I could go play outside with my animals. I had rabbits, pigs, chickens, horses, and the usual dogs and cats that reside at most farms and ranches. I was definitely no "girly girl," and, unlike Becky, I preferred the outdoors. This was our normal routine during the school year. During the summer months, we were just left at home alone most of the time—the six of us, three boys and three girls.

My dad worked for the county road department, in addition to his ranching, and he usually got off work around 4:00 p.m. each day. He would have preferred being a full-time rancher, but he simply couldn't make enough money at it to raise six kids. He typically drove directly to the pasture to check the cattle and feed them. Depending on the season or the time of year, he would check for new calves and do all of the necessary things a rancher has to do. In the winter, he had to break ice, which usually took longer.

Once in a while, during the winter months, he would stop by the house on his way to feed the cows and build a fire. He would stoke it enough that there would still be hot coals by the time we kids got off the school bus. However, many times, I came home to a freezing cold house in the winter. The old wood stove was the only source of heat in the entire two-story house, and my mom insisted that the house be warm for her when she got home. Usually my brothers would build the fire, but oftentimes they didn't ride the school bus home because they hung out with friends after school. They were several years older than me, and, by the time I was eight, my oldest brother was already married. I began building the fire when I was about seven. Looking back now, I realize that I was one of the original "latch key kids"—before the term was ever coined. Still, this didn't seem unusual to me, and I thought nothing of it. In fact, I was rather proud of the fact that I did things that other kids weren't allowed to do. I saw myself as being a responsible child. The truth is, I was beyond my years in responsibility, yet maturity and responsibility are not the same things. Little did I really know how stifled my maturity truly was. I had no real guidance or boundaries; there was no nurturing or appreciation shown me. There were just chores and expectations, while my mother demanded respect. There was no such thing as a weekly or monthly allowance in my house. I always felt that I was "earning my keep."

My mom usually got home around 6:00 p.m. after having gotten off work around 5:00. There was rarely an enthusiastic greeting and never a hug or affection of any kind. There was never a question about how my day had gone. Mom usually entered the home with a sigh and the acknowledgement that she now had to prepare supper for everyone. What a drudgery after having spent her day as a secretary surrounded by people she enjoyed and feeling a sense of pride in her work and that she was needed! She didn't seem to enjoy being a wife or a mother, and I picked up on her attitude at a very early age. She would make comments to my dad that she surely wished that she could stay home with the kids like many of her relatives, but she couldn't because he didn't make enough money to support them. This used to hurt my heart when my mom talked in such a derogatory way to him. I was pretty perceptive as a young kid, and I was sure that my mom would not have wanted to be a "stay at home mom." She enjoyed her life as a secretary. She loved her job and the friends that she had made. It seemed to me just one more way of hurting my dad's feelings and rubbing in that he wasn't a good provider. She didn't seem to like him very much. Sometimes it seemed that she hated him.

Most days when I got off the school bus, I was very hungry, but I knew that food was scarce in the house. Snacks were never available. Like a lot of kids, I craved junk food. Thinking back about our refrigerator, I remember that the handle didn't work, and I have wondered sometimes if my parents didn't take the handle off just to keep us kids out. I was pretty clever though, and I remember sliding a chair up to the door and prying it open at the top with a butter knife. I remember being very careful to take only items I knew my mom wouldn't notice missing—like one slice of cheese or one slice of lunchmeat or a sliver of a leftover.

I couldn't wait to get my hands on that candy bar reward that evening, and I anxiously waited for the headlights of mom's Nomad station wagon to pull into the yard. I was very aware that how the rest of the evening would go depended on how well my mom's day had been, and that thought caused me a lot of anxiety as a child.

My dad rarely got home before 7:00 p.m., and, when he arrived, he would come in the house looking tired and bedraggled. He would wash up and go sit at the supper table awaiting whatever Mom had the time or energy to prepare. Then, after supper, he would read the evening newspaper and fall asleep in his recliner. This was the usual routine in my home when I was a youngster.

On this particular occasion, my dad hadn't gotten home yet, and, immediately, the vision of my mom flashed before my tear-filled eyes as I recalled the angry tone in my mom's voice.

"You call this clean? What exactly did you do after school today?" my mom barked. I remember how my little heart sank as I watched my mom flop down on the couch, flinging the newspaper from her hand as she reached into her oversized purse and pulled out the Hershey Special Dark chocolate bar. Slowly, she peeled the wrapper back from the candy and proceeded to bite into it, smacking her lips and pointing out to me just how delicious it tasted. "If you had done your job, you could have had this candy bar," my mother sneered. My heart began to break all over again at the reminder of just what a "bad girl" I was. I wanted my mother's approval so desperately, yet I secretly hated her guts at the very same time.

"Conditional love!" I said to myself, as I became aware of my surroundings in my recliner. Now my audible words became thoughts again as I realized that this is exactly what my therapist had talked about during previous counseling sessions. I shared several traumatic experiences I went through at the hands of my mother, and each time an experience came up, my therapist reminded me that my mother's love was conditional.

It seemed that the only affection, warmth, or approval I ever received was entirely dependent upon my fulfilling the high expectations of my mother. Love was based on performance, and, if I did not perform to my mother's high standards, I simply was not good enough; I was not worthy or loveable. This was the lie that I had believed for so long. I now realized just how incapable I was of being the perfect little girl my mother demanded me to be. Retraining my brain to believe I am truly loveable and worthy was going to be quite a job. There would be no way of knowing how long this healing process would take. But I was willing to find out!

    I praised God that I had a dad who made me feel worthy, important, and loved. Thanks to my dad, I did the best I could to give my sons the affirmation they needed. I tried to compliment them and be proud of them. I hope and pray that the love I showed to them was not as conditional as that which my mother showed me. I know I could have done better, but—thank the Lord—I was not as mean to my children as my mother was to me. I fear, though, that some of these learned behaviors were passed on. I suspect that some of my grown son's issues stem from fears they had of me. I was absolutely terrified of my mother. It would only stand to reason that I transferred some of my anger and mean disposition onto my poor helpless children in much the same way that my mother had done to me. God, help me, and forgive me for the wrongs I committed against my precious children! I pray that they can forgive me too.

Chapter Notes and "Aha" Moments :

Chapter 10

More Tragic Memories

Staring at my messy desk, I felt such a strong compulsion to reach for my Bible. I felt the need to find scriptures that would validate me as a child of God. I was beginning to see that, in spite of my own mother's hatefulness, I had the love of a far more important Being than my cruel, earthly mother. I had the love of the Savior of the universe, and my sadness of being loved solely for my performance seemed like a million miles away.

"I have loved you with an everlasting love." I flipped through my Bible to get to the concordance where I quickly found these words in Jeremiah 31:3 in the context of: "The LORD appeared of old to me, saying: 'Yes, I have loved you with an everlasting love; therefore with lovingkindness I have drawn you.'" As happy tears began to form in my eyes, I now remembered the text in Psalm 139:13 and 14, which says: "For You formed my inward parts; You covered me in my mother's womb. I will praise You, for I am fearfully and wonderfully made."

I suddenly remembered my therapist telling me how important it was for me to take time to nurture my "little Marie." She told me that I needed to think about my younger self and identify who she was and what she looked like, and to try to understand why such an innocent little girl would be filled with such fear, anger, pain, and hate. She also wanted me to visualize Jesus holding me as a child and protecting me so that I could let it all go and let myself finally "grow up" and mature to the adult that I am today.

Psychologists have concluded, with much research to back their theories, that a child becomes stifled, or stuck, at the age of his or her early trauma. In other words, when a child is traumatized, there is an interruption in the ability to mature, and they become stuck at that maturity level, though they continue aging. When a "trigger" comes up for adults and they are retraumatized, they tend to shift back to the maturity level of the age at which they were traumatized. In my case, I was traumatized from conception on, so there really is no starting point for me. It is almost as if I've had to begin at the very beginning. When the phrase "born again" is used, I have often thought that I have literally had to be "born again" in the truest sense of the word. Nicodemus wasn't too far off in his questioning of Jesus in wanting to know how a person could be born again. Sometimes I feel as if I am living proof that one can indeed experience being born over or reborn.

There, sitting in the dirt by the hay barn, was "little Marie." My blonde hair was a dirty mess, and my face was filthy. I watched the chickens as they scratched in the dirt, and I felt a warm gust of wind on my cheek. *I wish I could be a chicken*, I thought as I daydreamed. They were so carefree and seemingly oblivious to life's problems, just pecking and scratching. Then, I remember looking up and seeing a Bald Eagle soaring above the large cottonwood trees across the bank near the creek. *I wish I could be an eagle!* I fantasized what it would be like, as I marveled at its majestic wings. Then, looking down, I saw the stains on my dirty tan pants from the dried urine. I had slept in those pants the night before and had wet my bed. It was a weekend morning and, as soon as I could, I escaped to the outdoors, not wanting my mom to see me.

> *I wish I could be a chicken, I thought as I daydreamed. They were so carefree and seemingly oblivious to life's problems, just pecking and scratching*

I had been wetting my bed for some time, and my mom was so ashamed of me. I recalled being scolded on many occasions. "Do you know how much it costs to wash those sheets every time you pee the bed? You stop that!" With each reprimand, she would tell me that I stunk. Oh, how I wished I could stop. I tried so hard to not have any "accidents," but nothing helped. I remember trying to stay awake all night just so I wouldn't pee in my bed. The only bathroom was downstairs next to Mom and Daddy's bedroom. I was too terrified of waking them up to go downstairs, and, during the winter months, I was too cold to venture out of bed. The only source of heat in that old two-story house was a wood-burning stove downstairs. We could literally see our breath. I had an electric blanket and I remember fearing that I would electrocute myself when I wet the bed. It didn't matter how badly I had to go; nature simply took its course.

Staring at the majestic eagle above me, I remember how I got up and climbed to the top of the loading chute which stood right next to the corral and the soft dirt that I had been sitting in. The chickens still scratched the dirt beneath me as I climbed up—up to the very top of the loading chute made of railroad ties. I remember that both of my feet fit perfectly on the top, and I continued to watch the Bald Eagle as it soared overhead. I remember balancing myself perfectly and spreading my little arms out as far as they would go. My face tilted toward the warm morning air, and I wanted to fly. I wanted desperately to soar like that eagle. I remember looking down from the dizzying height of the loading chute and thinking to myself, *I should jump, though I might die, but I could end how much I hurt!* Then, shaking myself into awareness, I realized I might only just hurt myself, and then I'd be in trouble. My adult Marie, now consciously aware of the memory, recognized how disturbing it is that a child so young could fantasize about ending her own life. That was me. I thought frequently as a child of ways of becoming invisible, of vanishing, of making it all go away. Oh, if I could have just crawled into a hole and disappeared.

Suddenly aware of my surroundings, there was a blackness, my breathing became heavy, and I felt hot as I looked into the rubber tub. There at the bottom, peeking out from under photo albums was my little blue stuffed horse. I recalled being under my blankets, crying and hurting. I was terrified, but as I thought about the incident, I couldn't recall what I was so afraid of. I was breathing hard because I had been trying to smother myself. I couldn't have been more than four or five years old. I held the stuffed animal over my mouth and nose and tried *not* to breathe. I wanted to "be gone." I just didn't want to *be*. I don't even recall which stuffed animal it was, but my little blue stuffed horse had triggered this memory. I currently felt a sick feeling in my lower stomach and in my private parts, and I sat and wept because I knew I was recalling a sexual trauma that had happened some forty-five years earlier. My body had remembered, and now my mind was reminded too. I felt so dirty and ugly and ashamed— always ashamed. I would later find out that this trauma was likely the reason for my bed wetting.

Then my mind floated back to another time and place. It was a school day, and I was sick. I hated being sick because I didn't want to miss being with my friends. School was the safest place for me to be, and I loved my teachers who seemed to have a genuine interest in me. As an educator, I can spot the children who have less than perfect home lives, and I suspect that most of my teachers were suspicious that I was not as well cared for as my mother would want them to believe.

I remember feeling that my mom was mad at me that particular morning because I was sick and unable to go to school and because I had interrupted her usual morning routine. As I lay on the couch in the early morning, I watched my mom preparing to go to work. This was when I was in somewhere around the second grade. My siblings had already left on the school bus. I remembered how my mom stood in front of the mirror to primp, making sure every hair was in place and her makeup looked just right. I recalled with sadness that my mom never seemed to care that I wore the same clothes I had on the day before. I was teased by my classmates, but I tried to ignore the ridicule. I never remembered my mom ever combing my hair or washing my face. I don't even recall owning my own toothbrush. In fact, I remembered the rare occasion of staying the night with a friend and having to fib that I had forgotten my toothbrush when my friend asked if I was going to brush my teeth before bed. I couldn't even understand why they brushed their teeth before bed. Suffice it to say, it wasn't my mother who taught good dental hygiene. I learned about hygiene in my health class in middle school. By then, I had so many cavities that I didn't want to smile. My dad said I looked like I was biting into a prune when my school picture came home because I would not smile but, rather, clenched my mouth shut so my rotten teeth wouldn't show.

I remember wonderful occasions of sleeping at a friends' home and having clean sheets and getting to take a bath all by myself—in clean water. As a child it was our routine to go to Grandma's house (my mom's mother) on Sunday afternoons to take a bath. She lived in town and had city water. Mom believed in conserving water and didn't want to feel indebted to my Grandma because of an increased water bill, so we still had to take baths in pairs. The cleaner kids went first, and Mom just added more hot water as the next couple went in. We, on the other hand had a well at our house, which went dry frequently. Water was a scarce commodity and one that we were forced to ration. I was absolutely terrified of running the well dry. Bathing simply didn't happen at home unless the cistern was full or there had been an abundance of rain that year. I do recall, however, my mother frequently bathed. Though she used very little water and it was a shallow

> *I knew right then and there that EMDR worked, and I've been a proponent of it ever since. Spiders have lost their power over me, and I no longer have a fear of them at all*

bath, she was the privileged one. By the time I was eight, there were only four kids at home.

On most occasions, when the well did pump dry, my brothers would force me or my twin sister to go down into the bottom of the pump house to turn the well off. One of the boys would accompany us to the pump house to make sure the job got done. My sister and I would bargain with each other or lie about whose turn it was. This led to many arguments. We would go to great lengths to avoid having to go down in that place to shut the pump off. "I'll do all the chores for a week if you'll do it!" was my plea. I even offered her money (though I didn't have much to offer). But I usually caved in when she cried and begged me to do it.

The pump house was about twelve feet deep and very dark. A hand dug hole in the ground lined with cinder blocks, it had a small triangular roof over the top of it. I would climb down the ladder through a maze of spiderwebs and, as soon as the pump switch was shut off, the light would automatically turn on. I'm not sure why my dad had it rigged this way, but the second the light came on, the spiders would begin to crawl, and there were hundreds of them! Granddaddy long legs they were. I remember begging and pleading with my brothers not to make me go down into the pump house. As I scurried up the ladder as fast as my little legs would go, the spiders would crawl all over me! It was an absolute horror for me. I was petrified! I remember my brothers laughing. They thought it was funny, and they would tease and tell me what a big baby I was. I can remember them taking gunny sacks with them, and, the second either of us came out of the pump house, one of the boys would wrap the gunny sack around us and roll us on the ground to get the spiders off. Or they would use the gunny sack to swat them off of us.

My spider phobia was actually how I found out that EMDR truly worked. When I was still married to my first husband, he knew instantly that I had seen a spider in the house when I would let out a blood curdling scream. He would come running from the garage, barn, or wherever he had been, fling the door open, and yell, "Where is it?" He always knew when I had encountered a spider. There was no question that I suffered from arachnophobia.

I remember telling about my experience at church one day, and the counselor friend of mine told me he had a technique that could help me overcome traumatic experiences like that. I brushed it off for a while, and then, after Ron and Beverly had moved and were no longer members of our local congregation, I began seeing him for EMDR therapy after the death of my mother. During one of my first sessions with him, the trauma of the spiders came up again. He used EMDR on me, and what a miraculous life-changing day that was! I knew right then and there that EMDR worked, and I've been a proponent of it ever since. Spiders have lost their power over me, and I no longer have a fear of them at all. It was a miracle!

Poor "little Marie." I wanted so desperately to take my therapist's advice and reach inside myself and hug that poor deprived little girl. My heart was breaking at the amount of negligence and the lack of concern that was given me as a child. I had to accept and reconcile myself to the fact that I was indeed an abused child. I knew that the past that I had buried for so long would all come out eventually, and I only prayed that God would be gentle in my transformation toward healing. I really needed to nurture and love myself and to see myself through God's eyes. Now I had to be convinced that I was all that the Bible said I was—fearfully and wonderfully made, loved with an everlasting love. I had to truly believe that I was so loved that God chose to send his only begotten Son that whoever believed in Him would not perish but have everlasting life. I truly believed in Jesus and wanted Him as my personal Savior.

There were no conditions placed on God's love for me, and I knew I needed to believe this new truth. The clichés I had heard all of my life now seemed to penetrate the part of my brain that needed to grasp the true meaning of love. And I recognized that the love I had been receiving from my precious husband was genuine. I no longer needed to question or doubt him when he told me that he loved me. My lack of trust in love seemed to disappear into the dark distance as I looked down and realized I was giving myself a full body hug. I was embracing "little Marie," and I was rocking back and forth telling her that she was loved. "You are safe now, Marie!"

During one of my previous EMDR sessions, my therapist had given me some suggestions on how to visualize myself walking with Jesus and seeing Him as my Protector. At that time, I visualized my "little Marie" sitting safely on Jesus' lap and, in an instant, "little Marie" looked directly into adult Marie's eyes and smiled. It was a safe, innocent, beautiful smile, and she had a delicate little white dress on, and her hair was gently combed, and her face was clean. Now, I, the adult Marie, wept tears of joy, and I could let it go. I could now be the recipient of unconditional love. I could now learn to love others with unconditional love. And what a liberating feeling that was!

I suddenly realized that I was given an assignment to write a letter to my mother. *Well, there's no point in putting this off*, I said to myself.

Reaching for a rubber tub in the corner of the den, I began looking for a particular notebook that I wanted to use and that I knew was in there. As I dug through, I stumbled upon one of my old photo albums with pictures of my mom and some of her relatives. As I leaned back in my overstuffed recliner, flipping through the pages, one photo that caught my eye was of my mom and my Aunt Peggy. My aunt was married to my Uncle Dale, Mom's brother. I stared into the twinkling blue eyes of my mother and contemplated her big smile as she had her arm around my aunt. Oh, how everyone loved my mother! How happy she always looked in photos and how contagious her laugh was when she was with her friends and co-workers! How was it that I had such a different picture of her? Who was this woman staring back at me? How could I love my mother so much and yet be so afraid of her and even have hatred towards her as a child? I placed the photo back in the album, and, putting the lid back on the tub, I went to my desk to compose my assigned letter.

How do I even start writing this letter to my mom? I wondered. *What do I say to her?* It seemed like an impossible task, but I knew I needed to stick with it while the emotions were all still so fresh in my mind. I feared that if I didn't do it now, I might never muster the courage to do it at all. Reaching for a pen on my messy desk, I smiled at myself. *This is MY desk*, I said to myself. *I can do what I want with it. It's okay if I don't clean it right now. I am still loveable—even if I have a messy desk or if I don't clean things up to my mom's standards!*

I sat back down feeling smug that I didn't have to clean the house for my mom anymore and that I didn't have a mother to judge my messy desk. Yet, I was also sad—sad that the reality was that I didn't have a mother. She had died too young.

Chapter Notes and "Aha" Moments :

_____
_____
_____
_____
_____
_____
_____
_____
_____
_____
_____
_____
_____
_____
_____

Chapter 11

Letter to Mom

My husband had plans to do some visiting of church members who were farmers. Normally I would go with him as I loved to ride in the big trucks and farm machinery with him. On that particular day, he had the opportunity to drive a combine and then haul grain in their semi-trucks. I knew he would be surrounded by all men, so I decided to stay home. I thought maybe today would be the day to finish writing the letter to my mom that I had neglected to finish just days before.

I thought I was mentally prepared to complete it, and, as I read what I had begun, I continued on, describing the details of the trip to Water World in Denver with my nieces. My attempts at small talk were clearly an avoidance tactic. The assignment given by my therapist was to tell my mother how I felt about her and the way she treated me as a child. The intent was to get to the bottom of my bigger issues, and I needed to be truthful and honest.

> *God please help me to heal. Help me tell my mom the truth about how she made me feel*

Though I knew my mother would never read this letter, it was clearly part of my therapy in letting go of the past and in expressing all the years of pent-up emotions that would further my healing process—including my ability to be able to forgive her.

I was terrified! I sat in my recliner with my notebook on my lap, and I prayed a quick prayer: *God please help me to heal. Help me tell my mom the truth about how she made me feel.* I had no sooner gotten the "Amen" out of my mind when I began to feel the fear of being alone as well as the fear of my mother, and then I drifted back to a terrifying day when I was only a child.

The rooster crowed, and the squeaky screen door shut abruptly on the porch as Daddy came in from doing the chores, his milk bucket in hand and humming as he closed the front door behind him. This was a usual morning sound that I found comforting. The smell of coffee brewing wafted up through the floor vent next to the chimney, and I was eager to go downstairs and greet the day.

It was the weekend, and there was no school that day. I looked forward to the Saturday morning cartoons on our old television set. A pair of pliers lay next to the TV so that we could pull the broken knob out to turn it on. Mom would normally yell, "Breakfast's ready!" and a big breakfast would await us. But something was different about this morning.

It must have been about money again, I remember thinking. At the beginning of every month, payday would finally come, and Mom would sit at the kitchen table and look over the stack of bills that lay strewn all over. I was too young to understand the concept of money. Yet, I knew that not having it caused pain for the entire family.

Daddy, oblivious to Mom's working on the bills was about to enter the house to a full-blown war instead of breakfast. As I was putting the same clothes on from the day before and tying my worn-out tennis shoes to go downstairs, it all began.

Mom erupted in some tirade that I couldn't quite make out, and the rattling of the metal milk bucket slammed into the sink with a loud thud. By the time the stairway door was open and I was entering the kitchen, I could see my dad bracing for war as Mom was screaming at him about the monthly bills.

"How are we going to pay all of these bills? You don't make enough money to provide for us!"

On and on she went—one hateful remark after another. He was yelling too and finally, in exasperation, he screamed: "If you hadn't had those last two!"

With that, my dad turned and headed toward the door, slamming it so hard it shook the mirror on the wall and nearly broke the glass in the door.

"We'll just get a divorce!" she screamed. My heart sunk at the thought of my dad not being home. What if he didn't come back? I ran out the door.

"Wait for me!" I screamed at the top of my little lungs as my dad sped up the hill and out of the driveway. "I want to go with you!" Gravel was flying and my little face was hot from running behind the pickup with tears welling up in my eyes and running down my dirty little cheeks.

I was a grungy little girl of about six years of age, and I was terrified of being left at home with my mother. My tattered hand-me-down tennis shoes could not help me run fast enough to catch up to my dad. I saw him looking at me in the passenger mirror, but he wouldn't stop. Defeated, I fell to the ground in a heap and wept. Sadness, sorrow, but, most of all, fear overwhelmed me as I felt so lost, alone, and utterly abandoned. "Take me with you!" I repeatedly cried. I felt as deserted as the dusty yard I sat in. I didn't want to go back in that house where my mom was still ranting and fuming. I have no idea how long I stayed outside, but I found solace in the barn with the animals.

When angry, my mom would slam the dishes around, and she would get really red in the face. She had the bluest eyes of anyone I had ever seen, and, when she was upset, her deep blue eyes stood out against the red face with such an intensity that it terrified me. I felt that she took her anger out on me specifically. She hated that I felt sorry for my dad. I remember her grabbing me by the hair once. She was screaming at me because I had taken my dad's side during one of their arguments.

"He's just trying to get sympathy, you brat!" she snarled, as she shoved me to the floor. I also remember how she would sit on the couch and pretend to cry while the youngest of the three brothers (seven years older than me) comforted her and took her side after some of the arguments between my parents. She was certainly gaining sympathy from my brother. I would follow my dad out the door and hang out with him in his leather shop or tag along as he fed the animals. Together we would make our escape from the chaos inside the house.

The realization that "those last two" was a reference to me and my twin sister haunted me all my life. It was more confirmation that I was not loveable. Even though my dad had made the comment, for some strange reason, I didn't hold it against him. I just remember being mad at my mom for starting the fight and for being so mean to my dad. I always felt that she hated him ... and me, and I never knew what either of us had done to deserve such harsh treatment. I did everything I could to make her love me. Apparently, my affection to my dad infuriated her. It was as if my dad and I shared a common bond—my mother's hate.

Shaken into the current moment, I looked down at my letter and began writing:

Why did you hate me, Mom? Why did you say I was ugly? Why didn't you comb my hair or hug me? Why did you love Becky but not me? Why didn't you ever help me with my homework? Why didn't you ever attend any of my school functions? Why didn't you care enough to check on

> where I was, who I was with, or what I was doing? I needed guidance and discipline! But I didn't need your anger and your cruelty! Why didn't you come to my high school graduation? Why …

I paused to reach for a tissue to catch the river of tears flowing from my furious eyes. These were tears of pain and anger and a release of fifty-plus years of hidden hurts just dying to get out. Running down my face and onto the paper were emotions from a child who was too ashamed to cry because I was "ugly" when I cried, according to my heartless mother. The tears flowed and flowed and flowed as I continued to write, uncertain of where the lines on the paper were. I didn't care, I just wrote:

> *The truth is, Mom, I am furious at you! I hated the way you were so mean to me and to Daddy. I tried to do everything I could to make you love me. I never held a grudge against you or criticized you. I honored you like the Bible said I'm supposed to do. I stuck up for you even when you were wrong. I don't think any of my siblings know that you moved up to the upstairs bedroom after Daddy's stroke. You told me you couldn't stand him anymore. You hated having to take care of him and that it would have been better if he died. I remember chastising you for your remark as I helped you move your recliner up the stairs so you could decorate the room the way you wanted it. You had a television set and a nice lamp. You used my old dresser and put pretty purple throw rugs next to your bed so your feet wouldn't be cold when you got out of bed. You even took a space heater upstairs so you could be warm. Mom, the entire time we lived in that house, we kids never got a space heater. If not for the electric blankets, we would have frozen to death up there!!! We could see our breath in the wintertime! You were the most selfish woman I've ever known in my life! And when Daddy needed you the most, you abandoned him. It was your way of punishing him for living wasn't it? I know his stroke changed him, and he became demanding of your time. He was even obsessive about your being five minutes late. But honestly, Mom, I think you got home later than you promised on many occasions just to upset him. You were horrible to him, and I resent you for it!!! I resent you for so many things! I hate you! I hate you! I hate you!*

My pen could barely keep up with the thoughts of anger that were spewing from my mind. As I remembered seeing her sitting in her recliner upstairs while Daddy was down in the living room, I recalled something about the doorway, and suddenly my pen fell to the desk.

I recalled the open doorway and then suddenly realized that Mom had hung a door so she could have more privacy. I was incensed at the thought that I grew up in that upstairs bedroom that I shared with my two sisters without a door and just across the stairway was the room that my three brothers shared, and their room had no door either. Then, an eerie, sick feeling came over my body, and my writing continued.

> *How could you not have known what was going on up there, Mom? How dare you pat Greg on the head and tell people what a good little helper he was. "While Joe and the other two boys are out working, Greg helps me take care of the girls," you said. You would tell people this with such pride in your little Greg. Oh boy, did he "take care of the girls." How naïve could you be to not pay closer attention when your little girls were surrounded by boys eight to ten years older? How could you leave us over at Uncle Fred and Aunt Milly's house? When we cried and said we didn't want to go, you just told us to shut up and kicked us out of the car. To this day I cannot stand the sound of a squeaky rocking chair or the smell of chewing tobacco because of what that old pervert did to me while I sat on his lap. You were a terrible mother!!! You were so self-absorbed that all you could think about was yourself?*

Physically shaking and feeling sick to my stomach, I had to stop my letter. I took several deep breaths. The tears had stopped, and now I was just plain mad. I sat staring blankly at the ceiling. I just wanted to write this one letter to my mom, and I didn't want to leave anything out.

"Don't forget to bring down the dirty laundry." I remembered how often my mother yelled that phrase up the stairs. Oh, if she only knew what dirty laundry really was up in those two upstairs bedrooms.

I won't bother going into the sordid details of what took place upstairs in that old white two-story house. But I was violated in more ways than I care to remember. Not just by my brother, who was nine years older, but also by my sister who was five years older than me. I have no idea what my twin sister may have endured or if she endured anything at all. I just remember defending her and trying to protect her most of the time. As I now wrote, it has been seventeen years since I've had any contact with my twin sister.

Suddenly, as if I were hovering over my own body, I recalled some of the horrors of the house I had grown up in. I remembered that my mom and dad would have parties from time to time when we were growing up. The neighbors were aunts, uncles, and cousins, and my parents would take turns with them having each other over to play card games. The adults would be downstairs, and they would shoo us kids upstairs to "play." I remember innocent games of hide and seek and tag and red-light green-light. But I also remember the games that I thought to be buried for a lifetime. I was between four and ten years of age at the time.

The trauma of the fainting game came out during an EMDR session in which I recall many of us kids being upstairs in our house. The mattresses were pulled off the beds and put on the floor. The bigger kids would stand behind us smaller kids, and we were instructed to breathe deep and fast as we were squatting next to the mattress. As soon as the bigger kids felt the appropriate amount of breathing had taken place, we were instructed to stand up very quickly. Upon standing, the person behind us would squeeze us from the back as hard as they could which would result in our fainting and falling forward onto the mattress. The purpose of the mattress apparently was to break our fall and silence the sound of our falling down. The adults downstairs were not aware that this was even going on. Once in a while, if we got too rambunctious, my mom would pound on the ceiling with her broom handle and yell at us to quiet down. But during the fainting game, there wasn't a lot of noise going on. What was going on though was too horrible for me to document.

I recalled during the EMDR session that I wasn't always unconscious during the fainting game, and I immediately remembered how I used to fake that I was unconscious. I pretended that I was so that I didn't have to deal with what was happening to me. I had actually blocked these incidents out and didn't recall them until these sessions with my therapist.

The traumatic experiences of the fainting game had been repressed for so many years. Exposure to pornography, witnessing the torture of animals, and so many other abusive acts that I witnessed or that were done to me caused the PTSD that is responsible for the years of my depression, rage, and overall heartache. But thanks to my Lord and Savior Jesus Christ and EMDR therapy, the majority of the traumatic memories have come out, and I cannot hide the secrets anymore.

I've been asked why I haven't pressed charges against those who caused this damage since there is no statute of limitations on child molestation and incest. The answer is, some of my abusers are literally dead, and some are just dead to me. I have no desire for any kind of relationship or reconciliation. I've forgiven them, but I will never forget. I have chosen to leave the toxic environment and the people in it.

I would like to take a moment to discuss my views on pornography and the detrimental effects it has on society. The topic has come up during health classes and life skills classes while I was teaching over the years. I am stunned by the "Just Do It" notion that has bled over into many aspects of society and especially to our youth. While I don't wish to be harsh or critical toward the Nike company, I do have a bone to pick with the mentality of the marketing companies who target our young people and warp the minds of our children by promoting a "Just Do It" attitude. This mentality tends to give people free reign to do whatever we want—anything goes. Children now believe the notion that they should "just do it." Sadly, I have been told by students that my way of thinking about pornography is outdated. Because I do not condone pornography, I discover that I apparently am the one that needs to "get on board" or that I am the one who isn't "cool." Or I hear, "Mrs. Pflugrad, you're such a prude!" The comment I struggle with the most is when a classroom of teenage students tells me, and I quote, "Everyone looks at porn!" It simply is not true! What we look at is a choice. The only part of their statement that is true is that, on occasion, I do *see* porn, yet it is certainly not of my own choosing. My eyes are continuously assaulted by billboards, commercials, and magazine advertisements that are nothing but pornographic. I do not want to see what seems forced upon each of us. When children aged twelve to seventeen tell me that pornography is okay and acceptable, I cringe. Some of these kids profess to be Christians. They do not see anything wrong with pornography because, I believe, they are not being correctly educated about it. There are many people like me who are repulsed by pornography, and they *choose* not to indulge in it.

I can assure you that the exposure I had to pornography as a child was not by my choice. I did not go looking for it. I was assaulted by it and then, because of it, the curiosity and feelings that arose from the exposure caused me a myriad of emotions that I should never have had to experience. It was confusing to me as a child. Shame, guilt, and self-loathing set in, and, of course, justification followed. Masturbation is a topic no one wants to talk about either, but it's real, and it is damaging. It too can become an addiction. The root of and bottom line is the complete inability to control a desire. In other words, it is lack of self-control. Just because something feels good for a few seconds or minutes does not mean that it is good for me or that I should "just do it."

The adults who choose to engage in lewd activities because they cannot control themselves really need to take a long look in the mirror. Perhaps you need to ask yourself: Is this something I can see Jesus participating in? Many believe that they are not hurting anyone by enjoying pornography. I disagree. You are hurting someone—YOU! Men and women, this is an unhealthy behavior, and it only leads to hollowness and pain. It is an addiction, and it is no different from drug or alcohol addiction. Research is proving that, in many ways, it is even more detrimental. The Christian publication *Covenant Eyes* has a plethora of information regarding pornography. Its website, www.covenanteyes.com, gives shocking statistics, facts, and quotations about pornography use. I strongly encourage readers to go to this website. You will be amazed. The website Covenant Eyes provides ways of protecting and filtering your technology from porn sites and inappropriate viewing material. It also provides resources and support for people who are struggling with porn addiction and want recovery and accountability.

Regarding our ability to show self-control, I would like to reference the scripture that has impacted me greatly—the one about the fruit of the Spirit in Galatians 5:22, 23: "But the fruit of the Spirit is love, joy, peace, longsuffering, kindness, goodness, faithfulness, gentleness, self-control. Against such there is no law." Just before these verses, Paul wrote in verses 16-21: "Walk in the Spirit, and you shall not fulfill the lust of the flesh. For the flesh lusts against the Spirit, and the Spirit against the flesh; and these are contrary to one another, so that you do not do the thing that you wish. But if you are led by the Spirit, you are not under the law. Now the works of the flesh are evident, which are: adultery, fornication, uncleanness, lewdness, idolatry, sorcery, hatred, contentions, jealousies, outbursts of wrath, selfish ambitions, dissensions, heresies, envy, murders, drunkenness, revelries, and the like; of which I tell you beforehand, just as I also told you in time past, that those who practice such things will not inherit the kingdom of God" (Gal. 5:16–21). This seems very plain to me. God wants us to have the fruit of the Spirit. These are the character traits that He wants us to incorporate into our lives. God implores us to refrain from the works of the flesh. This is a work in progress, and I wish I could say that I have mastered them, but I haven't. I keep them in mind and diligently strive to avoid the works of the flesh each and every day.

Shaking myself back into the present, I took a look at my surroundings. I was in a safe place now. I reminded myself of my home, my husband, the fact that I was miles and years away from the past that had kept me paralyzed, or "stuck." I picked my pen up to write my final remarks.

> *I'm sorry you died, Mom. I'm sorry I didn't get to say good-by. I'm sorry I didn't get to tell you how I felt in person. I'm trying to forgive you, Mom. I'm trying to heal and make sense of all of this, but…*

Putting my pen down and looking around me to make sure I was grounded in the present, I noticed how exhausted I was. I had no idea that writing this letter would be so mentally exhausting. I wasn't finished yet and didn't feel that I could go on. Instead, I reached for my journal. I felt the need to document the progress I had made today. I was proud of myself for being able to calm myself down after such an emotional few hours. Just months before, when having traumatic thoughts, or triggers of memories like the fainting game, I would have gone into a full-blown anxiety attack that would have lasted for days. I couldn't wait to share my progress with my therapist and with my husband.

As I've already shared, my dad was certainly no saint. While I did feel a stronger connection to him, I can't leave out details of the damage he caused me. Just what is a "father"?

Chapter Notes and "Aha" Moments :

Chapter 12

Forced to Be Tough

When I think of my dad and my relationship with him, I think of how I envision God as my heavenly Father. A father is such an important figure in all children's lives, but, for a daughter, it seems even more important. Research has proven that our relationship or view of God can be heavily influenced by the relationship that we have had with our earthly fathers. No wonder it was difficult for me to put trust in God. Though I respected and reverenced my dad, he did not protect me. In fact, he was absent most of the time. My mother was the disciplinarian, and my dad passively ignored what was going on. I wanted a hero. I wanted a strong man to protect and shelter me. Since he really had no fatherly example and was raised by his mother and a grandmother, my dad simply didn't fully understand the role of a father. I don't hold that against him though.

I've always been perplexed by the humility and gentleness I've read about my Lord and Savior Jesus Christ. Because of the trauma of my childhood and the dysfunction I lived through, there had been a disconnect in my way of thinking. As I continue going through the daily sanctification process, I am finally recognizing that being a kind, loving, gentle, humble person is what is expected of us as Christians. This way of thinking was so contrary to my upbringing, and it's taken me years of self-discovery to be okay with being

> *My inner child had built a protective barrier that allowed me to dissociate myself from what was going on to be able to maintain a normal outward life separate from the damaged child within*

kind and loving. Deep in the recesses of my damaged brain, there was a belief that I had to control. It was the belief that I couldn't let someone's rudeness, criticism, or even opinion go unchallenged. I was defensive about everything and everyone. I had a built-in cynicism and protective layer that had built up like a callous. Because of the modeling of both of my parents and the lack of structure and nurturing as a child, I had to raise myself. Who else could I trust? My belief was that *I* had to be in control of everything. My inner child had built a protective barrier that allowed me to dissociate myself from what was going on to be able to maintain a normal outward life separate from the damaged child within.

As a result, I learned to control everything around me as a means of protecting myself because everything around me was so out of control. In learning to trust God, I had to lay my defenses down and surrender my will. I discovered that the strong will that I had used to protect myself for so many years was no longer necessary. I had to acknowledge God as my Defender and Protector, and I needed to believe fully that He wants me to surrender all of my emotional baggage to Him so that He can heal me fully. Giving up control meant letting go of a part of my identity, and I was having a severe identity crisis! Unfortunately, I still slip back into old behaviors, and the Holy Spirit gently nudges me and helps me recognize my character flaws. Sanctification is the work of a lifetime.

Being tough was a false concept that was very deeply ingrained in me. I was taught that crying or showing any weakness meant that I was a coward. I was made to feel ashamed if I showed any sensitivity at all. Even toward the animals, there was to be no compassion. They were just ranch tools. I have to remind myself that I am an adult now (in my 50s) and I have to give myself permission to acknowledge that my dysfunctional family was wrong. My parents are dead and buried, I am a thousand miles from any of my family, and they no longer have any influence over my decisions to be a good, kind, loving, Christlike individual. I actually enjoy being around gentle, kind, humble people now. I've learned to love and accept that angry little girl inside of me. I've given her permission to be mad, and she has lost her need to be angry.

At one point in my life I was actually repulsed by people I saw as weak cowards. I saw them as doormats and cringed when I saw them not stand up to someone. Now, I admire people who are able to stand silently while others act foolish and irrational while they meekly walk away, holding their head up because they didn't have something to prove. It is an admirable quality that I hope and pray will become one of my good character traits through repeated practice. A very dear friend of mine told me about a statement attributed to Abraham Lincoln. His words impacted me tremendously: "It is better to remain silent and be thought a fool, than to open your mouth and remove all doubt." Thank you, Darrell, for the advice. You exemplify this quote, and I'm trying!

My dad was not a fool. He was a meek and humble man. However, he did not approve of some of the people that I admired. He was quite critical and judgmental of those he saw as "weaklings," though he may not have known much about them at all.

I remember as a child looking forward to watching "Mr. Rogers' Neighborhood" when I got off the school bus. I would run in the house and catch the tail end of Sesame Street, and then Mr. Rogers came on. I hid my secret affection for him because, on the rare occasion that my dad would come in the house and catch me watching it, he would make sarcastic remarks about what a "prissy" man Mr. Rogers was. He would ask why I would want to watch someone like him. When I heard my dad coming, I would quickly turn the television off. I didn't want my dad to be disappointed in me and judge me based on his feelings toward Fred Rogers.

There was just something comforting about Mr. Rogers' demeanor. He was always kind, gentle, and friendly. He seemed genuine, and it was as if he were speaking directly to me when the camera would close in on him. He would look right into my eyes and say, "You are very special, there is no one else just like you." It really sunk into me that I was an individual, despite the fact that I had an identical twin sister. He made me feel special. I didn't care that he wore goofy sneakers or that he changed his cardigan sweater every day. I didn't even mind his repetitive songs and quirky voice. He was predictable, and I desperately wanted consistency and structure.

I was such a tough little girl—I had to be. It wasn't that I wanted to be, or that I was even proud of it. I just had to be. I had three older brothers and an older sister. The boys were just plain mean. Known as "the twins" or "the little girls," we were just an annoyance to them. From my earliest recollection, I was told that we were unwanted. We were an accident. The reason Mom and Daddy didn't have enough money was because they had us. There was never an ounce of compassion in my childhood. I was rarely called by my name; my brothers would call out "babies" or "twins" when they wanted our attention. We were just one person in their mind because we were always together. So, we came running at their beck and call like dutiful little servants. "Get me a drink,"; "take off my boots"; "put some wood in the stove." There was never a "please" or a "thank you." We were always just bossed around.

If I got hurt, I'd better get over it quick. Mom had no patience for "cry-babies" or "sissies." If we were bleeding, it better be a bad wound, otherwise, her comment was, "Quit crying; it's a long way from your heart!" A band-aid and some peroxide or Merthiolate would cure anything, and, regardless of how much it hurt as they poured or dabbed on the red ointment, I could not allow myself to cry. My dad was a little more compassionate when I was hurt, but he still made comments insinuating that I needed to "toughen up."

In the second grade I tripped and fell on the playground while chasing a bully away from my sister. I had a two-inch laceration below my knee which I kept hidden until blood ran out of my pant leg and onto the classroom floor. The teacher spotted it and rushed me to the office. My mom was called, and I was taken to the hospital where eleven stitches were put in my leg. Instead of compassion, my Mom scolded me all the way to the doctor. She was upset that she had to take time away from work. I don't recall shedding a single tear during the entire incident. The scar remains to this day as a reminder of my "toughness." My sad reality.

All-Star Wrestling was a big thing in the 1960s, and every Sunday evening it would come on the TV just before Mutual of Omaha's Wild Kingdom and the Wonderful World of Disney. Daddy would watch the wrestling matches, and he would sit on the floor in front of me, and I would give him a "chiropractor treatment." I'd "work on his back," as he called it, and we would all sit and watch the professional wrestlers on TV.

I recall the glares my mom would give me as I rubbed my dad's shoulders and neck. Looking back now, and, after having some therapy sessions regarding family dynamics, I can see now that my mother was very jealous of my relationship with my dad. It was a very sick and twisted role reversal that went on in my home. My mother's skewed thinking, because of her dad's treatment, obviously affected her thinking about the relationship my dad and I had. My dad never abused me sexually, yet my mom projected her hate for her dad onto me. This was an amazing revelation to me during an EMDR session.

The wrestling on T.V. was only simulated fighting and just for entertainment, but I thought it was real. Daddy and I, Tommy, once in a while Becky (when she wasn't playing with her Barbie dolls), Bill and Greg (if they were around) would gather in front of the "boob-tube" to get our weekly fix.

I learned all kinds of wrestling techniques and maneuvers like the figure 4 leg lock, the sleeper hold, the scissor drop, the piledriver, the full Nelson, the half Nelson, and of course, how to pin an opponent. Tommy would have me practice them on him, and he too, would practice on me. He'd make me yell "uncle" once the pain got more than I could endure. I knew all the names of the important wrestlers. There was Man Mountain Mike, the Butcher Vachon and Mad Dog Vachon (also known as the Vachon Brothers), Andre the Giant, and others that I have since forgotten.

My two oldest brothers, Bill and Greg, who were eleven years and nine years older than I, respectively, would have friends over, and they thought it was funny to have "All-Star Wrestling" in the living room. They only did this when my parents weren't around. There would be Bill, Greg, Tommy, and several friends—sometimes up to six people in the living room. They made a pretend ring and would force me and Becky to wrestle. Sometimes a large sheet was placed on the floor identifying the boundaries that we could not go beyond, otherwise we would be penalized for "leaving the ring." They thought it was "cute," but I hated it.

Being identical twins, we were very evenly matched, and we would start out with just simple wrestling moves. If we got tired and tried to get away, they would push us back into the "ring." They were the "turn buckles," and when we got to the edge of the imaginary ring (that is, off the sheet), they would shove us back in. Our wrestling almost always drew blood. This was the secondary purpose for the sheet. It would catch the blood that dripped from our mouths, lips, and noses. We weren't allowed to fight dirty. No slapping, biting, hair pulling, or scratching was allowed. It was strictly kicking, hitting with fists (also known as knuckle sandwiches), or putting each other in holds to the count of three. Tommy was usually the designated referee. He got to declare the winner and would hold the winner's hand up high, just like on the TV show.

There were times we would be so exhausted that we would beg them to let us stop. I remember even giving up and letting Becky win. We took turns and sometimes even planned ahead of time who would give up first so we could get it over with. We had to be secretive about it because they would make us wrestle until *they* had had enough. *They* got to decide when we would quit.

They would even place bets on us, and, if we didn't perform to their standards, they would make us fight until they were completely satisfied or until the blood needed to be stopped from getting on the carpet. I even remember them making me put toilet paper in my nose to stop the blood so I could go back and fight some more. They even gave us names. Bill called me "Fats" or "Tubs." I don't remember what they called Becky. All my life I've been heavier than Becky. "In the blue corner we have 'Fats,'" the announcer would say, "and in the red corner we have [whatever they called her]." Then they would say, "Ding, ding, ding," to indicate that the bell had rung and the competition had begun.

We would go to the center, shake hands, and then "let the wrestling begin" or "come out fighting." I didn't realize until I was in my forties that this was a form of abuse. I hated doing it, even though I got a lot of praise and accolades for being so "tough." I got to where I would hide or go up in the hills when the boys came home with friends. I remember them yelling my name to get me to come to the house. But I'd hide or run as far as I could to get away. This took place from the time we were about five until we were probably about eight. Once Bill got married in 1972, it pretty much ended. I remember some of their friends even feeling sorry for us and telling them to let us stop. They would say, "I've had enough; let them quit." I remember the looks of pity on their faces. I'm sure they remembered for a long time and even talked about the little twins and the All-Star Wrestling they witnessed. It was traumatic, but I didn't know it at the time. All I knew was that I got praised for being so tough. I loved to impress them, but, at the same time, I felt horrible when I saw Becky bleeding, or, when she would get the better of me, I would get mad, and our little wrestling matches always ended up with us mad at each other. Anger, anger, anger—always anger!

There we were, enjoying an ordinary day, playing and having fun, or laughing—whatever we happened to be doing. Then suddenly, here came the boys with their friends, and Becky and I were summoned to the living room for "All-Star Wrestling." The next thing we knew, we were being subjected to this torture that sometimes lasted over an hour. It lasted until they decided they were done. I was forced to fight with my sister for no reason. I wasn't a fighter by nature. I was a tender-hearted little kid. This made no sense to me, and it was kept secret from our parents. I once told my mom about it when I was in my teens, and she laughed and told me I was exaggerating. I never brought it up again, and I hadn't thought about it until recently.

For some unknown reason, I was very sensitive and compassionate. In reading my baby book as an adult, my mom had written that I was such a "sweet baby, that I went around telling everyone 'I sawwy,' " meaning that I was sorry. I was protective of my twin sister. I knew I was older, only by 17 minutes, but still I saw her as the baby of the family. We were identical twins, yet I felt very different from her. She liked dolls and dressing up. She wanted to be pretty and primped a lot. I had no use for any of that.

I wanted to be outside with my animals, and she would beg me to play house with her or to play with her and her Barbie dolls. She even offered to pay me to play with her. Looking back now, it might seem funny, but the truth is that she used her dolls as an escape from the reality of the dysfunction going on in that home as much as I retreated to the outdoors and my pets as my form of escape. She was still playing with her Barbie dolls in her makeshift cardboard Barbie house at the top landing of the stairway until she was fifteen.

This is just another example of negligent parents and some of the things that can go on in a household where there is no supervision or the supervision is that of the abusive older siblings. It's kind of like putting a fox in charge of the henhouse.

My high school years were fraught with meanness, and I hung out with a tough crowd. We had a reputation, and I lived up to it. I am ashamed today of who I was and the inherited reputation I had by merely being the younger sister of my brothers who were not to be messed with. In a strange way, my adolescent experiences did come in handy in dealing with and identifying with the youth of today. There is very little that I hadn't tried, and the students I taught could rarely pull anything over on me. So, from that standpoint, I have to say something good did come from my bad adolescent years. I did survive, and when I found Jesus at the age of nineteen, I was finally ready to change. I tried to be a good example for my sons, and I was able to stay a step ahead of most of their adolescent antics. They have no real clue as to what their mom's history was. I wish I could forget most of it, but at least I have the promise of forgiveness. I've repented, and the promise is that my sins have been cast to the depths of the ocean, and that is where I hope they remain.

I wish I could forget the fights I witnessed between my older sister and the youngest brother. They were only two years apart in age, and, when they fought, I was truly traumatized. My older sister was the meanest, dirtiest fighter I've ever known. She would grab anything she could get her hands on, and she meant business. Their fights always started with an argument and name calling, and it quickly escalated. One particular day I was sure she was going to kill him, and she would have if he hadn't gotten out of the house. She threw a hatchet at his head, and it landed in the wall just inches from his head as he was running out the door.

On another occasion, she tried to stick his head in the oven while my mother was baking something. The last significant fight I remember them being in was in the kitchen while my mom was ironing clothes. She tried to get them to stop fighting, and she got in between them when my sister grabbed mom's hot iron and went after my brother's face. My mother stuck her arm in between his face and the iron, and she was burned badly on the back of her arm. The scar would be there the rest of her life. I was thirteen years old when this happened. This was just normal life for me. I lived in a constant state of fear my entire childhood, and, somehow, I thought this was normal.

I remember coming into the living room to a ruckus when my sons were about six and eight. They were in the middle of a wrestling match that had turned into an all-out fist fight. Flashbacks of my younger days flew through my mind, and I remember breaking them up and making them apologize to each other once I found out why it started. Their fight had also just started as horse play, but it had escalated to the point of pure, ugly hatefulness. I did not ever want to see that again. To this day, I have not seen them in a fist fight, and I pray I never will. I am grateful that my sons are close and that they didn't have to witness the kind of violence I was raised around.

My son, the Marine has witnessed more violence during wartime than anyone should have to see. But he doesn't like me to talk about it. So, I don't. Violence is ugly no matter where it comes from.

Unfortunately, my sons have been tainted by society's expectations of what true manliness is. The notion that a man must be tough or that he isn't a man is complete hog wash! I fear that they see Jesus as a prude and a coward, and they've even expressed that they don't understand why Jesus would let people put Him on the cross if He were truly God. "Why didn't He defend Himself?" they've asked. This is a concept that many people struggle with. Trying to get young men to understand meekness and gentleness as a strength goes completely contrary to all that they see in the mainstream media. Movies are full of violence, and, even though the good guy sometimes wins, he is still portrayed as a crude, rude Neanderthal. Then, for some sick reason, our young ladies want to have some big "lunk" of a man rescue them and drag them off into the sunset. Heaven forbid that a kind, gentle man could possibly rescue a woman by using wit, charm, and his own good character to woo a young lady. Many of today's young women would be turned off by this, and, until they've been beaten, abused, and treated like dirt enough times to come to their senses, they'll remain faithful to the abusive idiots. They'll wholeheartedly believe they can change him. How dare I speak this way of our young ladies, you ask? Well, I was one of them. Fortunately, not all girls are like this.

I praise the Lord that I have a wonderful, gentle, meek but very strong godly husband today. He is my rock, and I find more toughness and strength in his silence than I ever did in the abusive men I dated that were loud, obnoxious, and full of themselves. My husband is full of God. He is a brave and strong man, and the only thing he fears is God, and that's exactly the kind of man I want. He is a God-fearing Christian man who loves me unconditionally. I no longer have to be tough. I choose to be kind and loving, and I'm still learning. I fully understand why Jesus allowed Himself to be crucified. I thank Him daily that He was! I am grateful for Fred Rogers, who was also a godly man. In many ways, Fred Rogers gave me more guidance through a television screen than my own parents, and I appreciated him.

My brothers will never recognize the trauma they caused me as a child. To them it was all in fun and play. I have accepted their stupidity and carelessness, and I have chosen to forgive them whether they know it or not. I am at peace with it now. I have also forgiven my dad who never understood what being a father really meant. In some ways, he was a meek and humble man, but he was very imperfect, and I still loved him in spite of his parental ignorance.

Chapter Notes and "Aha" Moments :

Chapter 13

Mom's Death

Dear Mom,

I have a lot on my mind, and I would like to share some of my thoughts with you today. I'm doing well, but I've recently had to get some counseling for some issues I've been having, and I just thought I'd let you know what I've been discovering. I'm so used to just dropping by the house when I have an issue or if I just want to let off some steam about one of my fellow teachers or if I'm frustrated with Jeff or one of the boys. I know that I could always share my thoughts and concerns with you. Somehow, before I would leave your house, I would feel better, rejuvenated and ready to face the next challenge. But not today, Mom.

You've been gone since July 9, 1999, and it is now 2015. So much has gone on since you died. There is no more Jeff. We got divorced in 2001, and I am now remarried. The boys have all grown up. Levi went on to pilot's school, and Sam joined the Marine Corps. He served for four years and is now a police officer. I have moved away and sold my cattle and am no longer ranching. I married a pastor, Mom. Will you be proud of me now? I got my master's degree and have taught special education for years. Are you proud of me now?

I took the girls to the water park, Mom, and we really had fun....

Suddenly, tears welled up in my eyes, and I sobbed as I recalled the day my life would be altered forever. It was Thursday evening, July 8, 1999. I had called my mom so I could give her a full report on what a fun day I had had with my nieces at Water World in Denver. I had taken my sons just weeks before, and my mom was mad at me for not having taken my nieces along. Always wanting to please my mom, I had promised her I would take them soon. So, after having dropped my nieces off at their home, I wanted to call Mom and let her know that we had gone and that the girls had had a really good time.

When she answered the phone, I began to tell her what all we had done. As I was in mid-sentence, she interrupted me to let me know that she was in the middle of an episode of *All in the Family* and that she hadn't seen that particular episode. "Just call me first thing in the morning. You can tell me all about your time with the girls then, okay?" With that she hung up the phone. I remember feeling a little deflated, but, *That's okay*, I thought to myself. *I'll just call her tomorrow.*

> "Just call me first thing in the morning. You can tell me all about your time with the girls then, okay?"

I had forgotten that I had to drive my fourteen-year-old son to the airport at 6:30 in the morning for a flight lesson. So, needless to say, I did not call her first thing in the morning.

This was before the days of people having cell phones readily available, so I just decided that I would call her after I got home. On my way back from the airport, I was met by an ambulance with lights flashing and siren blaring. As I pulled to the side of the road, suddenly my husband pulled up next to me and yelled at me to put the boys in his pickup and that I should follow the ambulance. Clearly expecting it to have been my dad, I asked what was going on.

"It's your mom, she fell and had an accident, they're taking her to the Pueblo Hospital."

After the boys were safely with him, I immediately turned my Ford Explorer around and tried to catch up to the ambulance. I was doing ninety miles per hour, and I couldn't catch it. I knew this had to be pretty serious, but I knew nothing else. As I pulled into the emergency room entrance, they had just unloaded her. I ran to the side of the gurney on which she was lying and saw that she was unconscious. Her head was covered in bandages, and they were rushing her into surgery. I was told that she had a brain hemorrhage, and they needed to operate immediately. I went directly to the waiting room and stayed until some of my other family members began showing up. My husband picked up my dad and brought him as soon as he could. My dad told me all about the events of the morning when he arrived at the hospital. He was so shaken up and inconsolable, and my heart hurt for him so badly. He felt completely helpless because he was. We all were.

It had been Friday morning, July 9, 1999, at about 8:30 a.m. when my mom decided to get some fresh air and do some mowing in the yard. My dad had had a massive stroke in 1997 and was now confined to a wheelchair. He had paralysis on his right side—the same side as his amputated leg—and he had very little function in his right arm. My mom had recently retired and was caring for my dad full time. He was still being fed through a feeding tube in his stomach, and I know my mother was burdened by him. She confided in me that she wished he just would have died. I remember her discussing funeral plans outside the I.C.U. when they were intubating him and how disappointed she seemed when he was revived. I remember being disgusted by her callousness but not necessarily surprised.

While in the Wal-Mart parking lot one afternoon, Mom was persuaded to take a little black mutt of a puppy home with her. It was a homely and obnoxious dog, and none of us thought she needed the extra chore. But she was convinced it would help keep her company.

On this particular July morning, while she was mowing weeds around the yard, that rambunctious little dog ran up behind her and jumped on her from behind, just enough to knock her off balance. She fell and hit her head pretty hard on the edge of the old push mower. My dad, in his motorized wheelchair was just 20 feet from her when it happened. He saw her fall and quickly wheeled to her side. She got up, and, when he asked her if she was okay, she said "yes" and went on to the house to begin preparing breakfast.

Within minutes of reaching the house, she mentioned to my dad that she didn't feel well and had a bad headache. She took some aspirin and sat on the couch. Within thirty minutes she began telling my dad that she thought he should call for help, she mumbled some words and then went lifeless on the couch. My dad dialed 911, but, because of the remoteness of the ranch, the ambulance didn't arrive for fifteen minutes. She was rushed to the hospital where they determined she had an aneurism from the bump to her head and was bleeding internally in her brain. They tried but could not stop the bleeding. She was rushed by ambulance thirty minutes away to receive care from a more advanced hospital, but it was too late. She never regained consciousness, and, because she had a health care directive, a "living will," in place, she was removed from life support. This was supposed to have taken place after seven days, but my oldest brother was not convinced that she was brain dead because of her involuntary twitches from time to time, so she was not then removed from life support.

On the ninth day of her hospitalization, the doctor removed all life support and two days later, at 6:07 a.m. on July 20, 1999, I was notified that she had just passed away. I've never experienced a hollowness like the death of my mother. The one I had tried my entire life to please was gone, and I didn't have the opportunity for any parting words with her. I had sat at her death bed and cried the day before she took her last breath. I begged God to forgive her for the hate she held in her heart towards her own dad. She had vowed that she would never forgive him for what he had done, and I wanted to intercede on her behalf. I prayed that God would forgive her for anything that could keep her from being saved for His kingdom. Only God knows what her heart was like at the time of her death. Even though she was "brain dead," I prayed that God could still reach her in her state of coma. Despite how angry I am or was at her, I had forgiven her and let her go, or so I thought. I had no idea how deeply ingrained her influence was on me or how I had allowed her to affect me and my life, my very identity and character—even after she was in the grave. I have since come to learn, through the EMDR therapy, that I was capable of letting go of the fears I had of her. When I was a child, she was the perpetrator in much of my abuse. My need to dissociate from that pain and still maintain a "normal" daily life caused me to stuff all the hateful emotions I had toward her. She is what is also called the "introject" for me. She programmed me to keep silent. There is an element of secrecy in abuse. Her influence was so strong over me that, after each abusive situation, I was made to believe that it was my fault. So, my little inner child took the blame and owned it for all of these years. Because I loved my mother, part of my inner child kept a loyalty to her, and the confusion I had between hating her and loving her at the same time caused such inner turmoil that it's no wonder I didn't handle her death very well. It wasn't until I was able to recognize these truths about how my inner child felt that I could reprocess the trauma and find healing.

I mourned the loss of my mother who I was very close to. Despite some friction, I always respected her and my dad. I never held grudges against them, and, even if there had been an argument between us, I was quick to find resolve and maintain a relationship. But the sudden shock of her no longer being there was too much for me to deal with on my own. She was so healthy, and she had just retired. She was a volunteer for the garden club and still had so much life to live. I found myself being angry at every little old woman I saw. I was mad that they got to live and that I would never see my mother age to see her have white hair like they had. I couldn't even look at the elderly ladies at church. This may sound very irrational, but it was part of my grieving process. It was the *anger* part of grief that I had to deal with. I wasn't mad at God. I was mad at the dog, mad at old women. I was mad at myself because I didn't call her. I didn't get to tell her about the fun day I had at the water park with my nieces. I was mad at her for leaving me, mad that she would never see my sons grow up, mad that I didn't get to tell her goodbye. The list of reasons to be mad can go on and on, but I was just plain angry. Anger was the story of my life.

With five siblings, it would have been nice to find support and comfort from them, but none of them could possibly understand my specific pain. Every person deals with grief in a different way. I was a spiritual person with specific beliefs about what happens to people when they die, and my beliefs did not match up with those of my siblings. It made it difficult to be around them, and I was sick and tired of being told that my mom was safe in the arms of Jesus. I knew the Bible truth, and my mother was simply resting in her grave. She knew nothing, and she certainly was not my guardian angel now, as they were telling me! According to the Bible, she was certainly not watching over me either. I just wanted them to leave me alone. I know they meant well, but they didn't have their facts straight, and it only made me angry at them. There are specific Bible texts that I reference. 1 Thessalonians 4:13-18 Paul states "I do not want you to be ignorant concerning those who have fallen asleep, lest you sorrow as others who have no hope...."

Another scripture verse that gives me hope is 1 Corinthian 15:51-55, which Paul also says "I tell you a mystery, we shall not all sleep but we shall all be changed, in a moment, in the twinkling of an eye... and the dead will be raised incorruptible...

Psalm 6:5 says: "For in death there is no remembrance of You; in the grave who gives You thanks?" Ecclesiastes 9:5, 10 says: "For the living know that they will die; but the dead know nothing, and they have no more reward, for the memory of them is forgotten. ... Whatever your hand finds to do, do it with your might; for there is no work or device or knowledge or wisdom in the grave where you are going." Then, Psalm 115:17 goes on to say, "The dead do not praise the Lord nor any who go down into silence."

The lack of support from my husband left me feeling alone and isolated as well. I wanted him to cuddle me, sooth my pain, help me to see that everything would be okay eventually. He had never lost a loved one, and I had. Maybe he thought I should have been used to it. But I wasn't. I just wanted him to love me through it, and he was not capable of that kind of love. He dealt with the loss of my mom in his own way. He stuffed his emotions—as usual.

Within six months I chose to separate from my husband of fifteen years. Hoping to get some resolution, I began seeing a marriage therapist and a grief counselor. Through all of it, I sought to find answers to my sadness and despondency, all the while, still maintaining a full-time teaching job and finishing up my master's degree. I was a very determined 35-year-old who thought that life would go on. After my husband admitted that he hadn't loved me for over ten years, I didn't really see the point in staying in a loveless relationship, though I was still willing to seek help. He had joined me for a few of the marriage counseling sessions, but, after about four of them, he informed me that it was my issue, and he didn't need any help. I felt even more lost and alone than ever, and his way of helping me was to just leave me alone. He left me to study, to go to college classes, and to work, while he took the boys on campouts and to auto races and football games. I'm sure he thought he was helping me, when I was actually starving for love. I was emotionally numb, but, as my workaholic mother had demonstrated all of her life, I poured myself into my teaching career and stayed busy working. After all, Mom used to use the quote, "Idle hands are the devil's playground." I wanted nothing to do with that.

I sat home alone on Tuesday morning, February 15, 2000, and wrote a long letter to each of my sons and one to my husband. I told my sons how much I loved them and that I was sorry that I couldn't be the mother they needed. I needed to be by myself for a while, so I would be moving out of the house.

I found a small modular home in a nearby town and moved some of my things out while they were gone with their dad. I cried the entire time I wrote the letters and sobbed as I packed my bags. I'll never forget looking through my rearview mirror at the home we had built together. Originally a 550-square-foot garage, we moved in and added on to it until it was the 2200-square-foot beautiful home I had lived in the past twelve years. The home sat on 105 acres right across from my family's ranch land, and it was to be where I would grow old and eventually be buried in the family cemetery just up the road. I saw our family dog, Bear, watch me drive away, and I hadn't even said goodbye to him. It was the saddest day of my life, and I was dying on the inside. Only God knows the true sorrow I felt as I simply gave up on what I thought was love.

Our divorce was very civil, and all I asked for was my maiden name. I left my sons with my husband, thinking that maybe we could patch things up. After all, we weren't fighting, there was no abuse, and no adultery going on. There was just no love left under the roof of what used to be a home. It was now just a house. My husband was the one who filed for divorce in June 2001, after he had begun seeing another woman. The divorce was finalized September 14, 2001, and I received but a fraction of my share of the value of the home he would sell later. I didn't bother fighting for it. I simply had no more fight left in me.

I had lost loved ones to death—grandparents, a favorite aunt, good friends, and countless pets as a child raised on a working ranch. I had even lost my dad to some degree. Though he was still alive, the stroke he had in 1997 had altered him so much that the big, strong rancher I had ridden with, gathering bulls just one week before his stroke was now a shell of a man. He sat in his wheelchair, crying uncontrollably because the stroke had changed his personality. I never dreamt that I would ever help bathe my dad, let alone have to give him enemas. But I was willing to do whatever was necessary to keep him in his home. Still, I never experienced a loss like that of divorce. This was an entirely different kind of loss—a loss that was compounded by the loss of my mother. Nothing could have prepared me for the sorrow and grief I was about to face.

My mother had been the glue that held the family together. As I look back now, I realize that the glue was a very sick kind of adhesive. She had a way of keeping everyone and everything running. She was very active in all of her children's lives and involved far more than she should have been. The reality was, she was extremely co-dependent. She was busy keeping everyone happy and mending fences for this child, smoothing the water for that, and meddling in the life of one of the others. I'm sure she meant well, but the truth was that, when a holiday came around, we all sat around acting as if we were a happy, fun-loving family, when the truth was that you could have cut the tension in the room with a dull butter knife. We kept the peace for Mom's sake. The secret disdain some of us harbored toward each other hung over us like a thick black cloud.

The outside world saw my mother as full of life, and, by everyone's account, she was the most loving, wonderful woman anyone could every know. She was a friend to all and had no enemies to speak of. Though inconsistent in attendance, she was a devout Lutheran who took some of her grandchildren to church on occasion. Two days after her funeral would have been my parents' 48th wedding anniversary. Everyone thought they had a wonderful marriage.

My mother had worked as an administrative assistant for twenty-five years and was very good at her job. The death of my mother shook the entire community and left my family with a huge void. There was no one around now to put out the fires and settle the disputes between the six children—six grown, adult children. The sudden shock of her absence and the shift of the family dynamics threw the entire family for a loop.

I'll never forget getting the phone call I received while at the hospital. My mother lay in a coma, and I was not going to leave her side. We already knew that the prognosis was bad and that she had been declared "brain dead." It was now just a matter of waiting for her to die. She had been removed from life support, but her vital signs were so good that she basically had to just shut down. While I sat at the hospital in prayer, begging God for a miracle, my brother was in a jail cell. The call came from my husband that the youngest of my three older brothers had been drinking and that he and his best friend had gotten into a fist fight. His best friend had him arrested. While in jail, my brother decided to take his boot laces off and hang himself. Fortunately, he was found and cut down before he died. So, apparently this was his way of grieving. But none of his siblings were impressed. This was one of the most selfish things I could have imagined. I was so angry at him. It wasn't enough that Mom was dead, but now he tried to kill himself. I always viewed him as my mom's favorite. Apparently, he couldn't cope with this loss. I am not the only alcoholic in my immediate family.

I can still remember when the sheriff deputy pulled up in front of the church to let my brother out of the patrol car so he could attend my mother's funeral. He was to be a pallbearer along with the other five of us. My twin had made the comment that, since our mom had carried all six of us into this world, it would be fitting for us six to carry her out of it. I thought it was a nice gesture. I just didn't expect one of her children, her favorite son, to have to be unshackled to do so. After the funeral was finished and her casket was covered, my brother was returned to his jail cell to finish out his remaining sentence. How pathetic it was—and yet not surprising—for such a sick and dysfunctional family.

I laid my notebook back on the desk and made my way upstairs. What a day it had been! Healing is hard work; I could not finish this letter now. I was too exhausted, and, as I thought about her death, it seemed as if it were only yesterday. I would have to visit this task some other time.

Chapter Notes and "Aha" Moments :

Chapter 14

Breakthrough Therapy Session

"Marie, you can come on back."

The comforting voice of the woman I had come to trust took me away from the questioning thoughts in my mind.

As I sat in the overstuffed chair, it was hard to keep my composure when the therapist asked, "So how are you today?" Tears began streaming down my face as my sorrow poured out over the reality of what I had learned and thought about and processed over the course of the last two weeks.

"I just don't know why she couldn't love me" I sobbed. "How can I love others when I can't love myself or see my own worth?" Taking a deep breath, I continued, "These rules or beliefs that I remembered and wrote down are all lies! I've been convinced for years that I'm stupid, ugly, worthless, and so many other things. They are all lies!" There was an angry tone in my remarks. I felt so betrayed by my own family and the dysfunction of my upbringing.

"Why did I think this was normal?" I cried mingled tears of anger and pain. "All my life, I've believed these lies on an unconscious level, and I was traumatized by them. On an intellectual level, I know I'm not stupid, ugly, or worthless. But, why am I so insecure and fearful? Why do I lack trust? Why am I so angry?"

I was beginning to see for the first time the truth of my life. The pent-up emotions were bubbling to the surface. The reality that things weren't as good as I once thought jolted me.

"My entire childhood was a lie!" It was as if a light had been turned on, as if a switch in my brain had been engaged.

The therapist sat listening as I vented my emotions, and she watched as I discovered and verbalized the answers to my own questions.

"These lies have to be re-framed or re-processed so that you can finally let them go," responded the therapist. "You have been through a lot, and I'm sure there is a lot more yet to find out. Our goal is to get you to change your previous belief system. You have to replace the irrational beliefs with the truth."

My therapist looked at me through genuine caring eyes, which caused yet another emotional outburst.

"I just feel hollow, empty, like I am a nothing or a nobody!"

My shoulders heaved as I tried to catch my breath in between the tears. I had an inkling that this session would be deep and powerful, but I didn't expect it to start from the very moment I sat down.

I always prayed before I went to each therapy session for God to reveal to me what He needed me to know in order to heal. I had no idea just what all would come up on this day, but it would be monumental.

"I know I'm loved by my husband, and I know my adult kids love me too," I cried. "I also know, on an intellectual level, that God loves me. But how do *I* learn to love me? I know I've made so much progress, and I have had a lot of resolve concerning the abuse I've lived through. I've even forgiven all of the things that have happened to me and those who abused me."

I began to sob again.

Leaning over in the chair now, I rocked back and forth. I remember feeling the need to lie on the floor or couch and curl up in the fetal position like I did at home during some of my worst anxiety attacks. My stomach was in knots, and I felt sick all over. But I just rocked and rocked.

"Who else do I need to forgive?" I cried.

Much of human trauma is felt in our physical bodies, and this was not a new sensation for me.

"Where are you feeling it the most?" asked my therapist.

"It's in my stomach, my gut, and in my chest. My heart hurts. I feel like my heart is breaking!"

She began to tap from one knee to the other as I slowed my rocking down.

Leaning as far over as I possibly could, I began to sob, "She didn't want me! She hated me! She wished I would never have been born!"

The gut-wrenching pain all came back to me as I recalled flashbacks of a conversation I had had years ago with a relative who revealed a truth to me that no one would ever want to hear. My mind flooded with questions and pain, as if my very soul was crying out into the blackness that was consuming me. I felt small, lost, hopeless, and powerless.

"What is coming up now?" asked my therapist, as she continued the tapping motion.

Just to recap—the tapping she employed is a sensory stimulant to aide memory recall from the recesses of the brain where trauma is stored. The tapping is often used in EMDR in place of having the eyes follow the fingers in a side-to-side movement or in place of watching the blue light go back and forth. In my case, I almost always closed my eyes during the most traumatic memories, so my therapist would use the tapping motion on my knees to obtain the bi-lateral stimulation.

Suddenly the conversation with my relative came back to me, and I shared with my therapist every detail I could remember.

"It was a cold November day, and my cousin came to visit me. It was in 2002. She lived out of town but came to town one day per week to work with students. She was a speech therapist. She knew I had gotten divorced and came to see me at the house I had recently purchased."

She very nonchalantly began reminiscing about our mothers. Her mother passed away about a year after mine. "You know about your mom trying to get an abortion when she found out she was pregnant with you, don't you?" she questioned.

I can still remember the exact location, the smell, the atmosphere of the visit. We were in the living room. There was a coolness to the air. Fresh paint and new carpet smells seemed to flood my senses.

> *Mom said your mom was so upset that she might have to have another baby*

I told the therapist: "I just let my cousin go on with the story. I didn't really remember responding to the comment. It seemed rather insignificant at the time." I looked off into space as my therapist was jotting down notes.

"My cousin continued, 'My mom told me your mom was really upset when she came to see her. She told her that she was afraid she might be pregnant again. She thought it might just be early menopause, but then when she started gaining weight, she got worried.' My cousin paused, as if she were watching my reactions. 'According to what my mom told me,' she continued, 'your mom decided to drive to a clinic in Colorado Springs (60 miles away) so she could find out for sure if she was pregnant. Then, if she was, she could have an abortion, and no one would find out about it.' There was still no response from me, so she continued, 'Mom said your mom was so upset that she might have to have another baby. She had three sons and finally had her daughter. Now five years later and broke all the time, she just couldn't bear the thought of another kid.' "

I recalled how I was a bit taken back by the information my cousin shared with me, but still gave her no response. After all, it was no secret that the family was as poor as church mice and that life was full of hardships and deprivation.

I had always been told that hardship makes people strong. "Being poor makes you appreciate what you have," Mom would say. I was quite proud of my accomplishments, given my meager beginnings. I didn't have a sense that my cousin was being hateful or callous. She was simply making conversation, and I remained silent and listened as she spoke—partly out of shock and partly from curiosity.

"My cousin continued: 'After the examination, the doctor apparently told your mom that she was indeed pregnant, but too far along in the pregnancy to have an abortion. He just sent her home.' "

Back in the 1960s there was limited access to ultrasound equipment, and the doctor had no idea my mom was carrying twins. He simply refused to perform an abortion.

This tidbit of information lay dormant in my mind for all these years. I hadn't thought about it until this very therapy session. I then remembered the hateful comments that my older sister had made, referencing me as "an accident" and that "I was Daddy's little girl until you came along. You weren't even supposed to be born!" It also revived the memory of my mom and dad fighting over money and the comment, "If you hadn't had those last two," which echoed in my ears like loud cymbals clanging together.

As she began tapping again, the therapist asked that I just relax and let my mind float back, "Take some deep breaths," she reminded me.

Suddenly a heavy weight came over my body, my shoulders tensed, and then my stomach tensed. Bending over and holding my stomach, I rocked back and forth. I was sobbing so hard I couldn't catch my breath. It is difficult to describe the feeling linking my body and mind. When I say, "gut wrenching," that is exactly what I mean. It was a feeling that is indescribable. Unless you've experienced this kind of emotional pain, I cannot expect you to understand it.

"Breathe, Marie," she stopped tapping. "You've got to breathe."

There was the longest pause … then finally came an exhausted deep breath and, again, the deepest sobbing with no sound coming out, but only the heart breaking and the soul in severe agony.

I cry as I write these words, just recalling the very emotion that I felt at the time. It's as if I relive it to some degree every time I read the story. It was a feeling of mourning, similar to the grief of losing someone. It felt like what I imagine death to be like—a hollow, heavy, oppressive, black hole.

Once this session was over, my therapist explained how this process of EMDR allowed me to actually drift back to a cellular level. I was able to experience the feeling of rejection in utero. It was the feeling at the very time my mother found out she couldn't abort me. She despised the pregnancy and the baby—me. It meant she hated me! My peace was disturbed from that moment on, and the impression of anger, bitterness, and resentment toward me, toward myself began. I could feel it all as a fetus; I could feel it! And now as an adult in my 50s, I could feel it all over again. I was re-living it. The imprint of rejection, hate, and the feeling of being unwanted, un-loved, and unlovable was coursing through my body and my mind—through my mother and her emotions. This became my identity from that moment on.

My years of sorrow and self-loathing all made sense to me now. If my mother didn't want me to be born and obviously resented me during her pregnancy, how could she love me at all? If my mother was angry through her entire pregnancy, and this anger transferred to me, then no amount of love shown me could replace the belief so deeply implanted into my identity while I was developing inside her. Even after I was born, the emotion was already locked into place.

Suddenly, unable to stop my body from shaking, my sobbing turned into more of a wailing. "What is coming up now?" she asked me in a serious tone.

The tapping had stopped, and she asked me to share what I was remembering. Flashes of jumping out of the upstairs bedroom window at the age of twelve came to mind. Deliberately driving myself off a cliff at eighty miles per hour while in a drunken state of pain and rejection at seventeen flashed before me. Wondering if I could die if I jumped off the top of the loading chute at eight years of age flickered into my mind. Then, nearly feeling the need to vomit, I shared with my therapist how, when I wasn't even five years old, I had tried to suffocate myself with my stuffed animal because I didn't want to live anymore. I wasn't old enough to understand death, yet I didn't feel that I should be alive. Somewhere in the depth of my being I felt I truly was not supposed to be alive, that the family, that life itself would be better if I were not here. It wasn't that I was suicidal, I simply didn't want to exist. I just wanted to *not be*.

Now, after recalling all of these incidents in what seemed like an eternity yet probably were only seconds, I sat stunned and dazed. Still sobbing, I asked my therapist, "Is it possible that my self-loathing could have begun while I was still in my mother's womb? Is it possible that my mother's anger at having to be pregnant with me could have impacted me while I was developing?"

I looked at the sympathetic expression on my therapist's face and could see the answer in her eyes—*Yes*. There was a pause and a deep breath. "This could very well be the answer you've been looking for," she said. "A mother's state of mind during pregnancy can significantly impact the development of the fetus in utero."

My crying slowed considerably as I took several deep breaths. The tapping came to a slow stop, and I blew my nose and wiped the tears from my face. My therapist just calmly helped me get re-grounded in the present as I looked around and became aware of where I was.

"It's not my fault," I said. "I didn't have any say in what my mother was thinking about her pregnancy. This was my mom's issue, not mine. My being born was not my fault!"

It was as if I had a fresh perspective. EMDR was at work and the "ah-ha" moment had come.

I suddenly looked directly in my therapist's eyes, and the words came from my mouth, "Jesus loves me, this I know." I began to cry a different kind of tear. I sat there feeling paralyzed, yet, oddly enough, I also felt liberated. A strong sense of peace and closure had come over me. It was a calm acceptance that I had never felt before. It was as if a gigantic weight had been lifted from me. It was almost as if a darkness had lifted and a light now illuminated me, as if a mystery had just been solved and a prison door had been swung open. There now seemed to be answers in the place of the nagging questions that had haunted me all these years.

"I can forgive myself," I smiled. "I can let go of the anger and the hate for myself for having been born." Another smile, and then almost a grin—"It isn't my fault! No matter how much my mom didn't want me, God wanted me, and He still wants me!" My therapist smiled back at me, nodding in agreement. Psalm 139:13 took on a whole new meaning for me; For You formed my inward parts; You covered me in my mother's womb.

"Let's re-process this new information, Marie, and get it locked into your brain so the shift can take place."

With that, I took a deep breath, and my shoulders lost their tenseness. I now saw myself in a new light. I had hope; I could finally allow myself to love *me*.

This discovery and awareness gave my mind the permission to reframe the emotions my mother placed on me. I suddenly had a new sense throughout my entire body, a new sense of my own self-awareness. A warm, almost floating feeling came over my body, and I felt light, secure, empowered, strong, and confident. My own emotional freedom to believe—for the first time—that I am lovable. I was wanted! I am worthy! God's truth is that He loves me and that He wanted me, and this is *the truth*—not my mother's beliefs. It felt like a re-birth. I forgave myself!!!! It was me who needed to be forgiven for being born. I now accepted the fact that it wasn't my fault! I had nothing to do with it.

I took the long way home so that I could have a little more time to decompress from this exhausting therapy session. My emotions ranged from sorrow to anger and finally resulted in peace and acceptance by the time I got home. I decided I needed to complete the letter to my mom that I had started several weeks earlier. Maybe it would be a little easier now that I had more clarity.

I've had the opportunity to do some research about the effects on a fetus in utero during pregnancy. In an article written by David A. Grimes titled, "Abortion Denied: Consequences for Mother and Child," published December 6, 2017, Grimes gives shocking statistics of research done over the years. It is not my intention to discuss abortion at all. This topic is about what happens to a fetus as it is developing, and I happen to be one of these statistics. It just stands to reason, and common sense would tell us, that a child who is born to parents who want it is going to be a happier baby. Obviously, then, a child who is unwanted would have the opposite feelings. Evidence gleaned from research concurs that unwanted children have a much greater risk of juvenile delinquency. These children most often are socially and emotionally disadvantaged. Studies show that children born after denied abortions suffer alcoholism, criminal activity, suicidal ideation, and overall psychological deprivation. I fully understand and believe that I am living proof of this research.

Chapter Notes and "Aha" Moments :

Chapter 15

My Last Letter

Dear Mom,

    I had an amazing therapy session today, and you were the main topic. During some of my other attempts at writing to you, I may have seemed a bit angry. I used some very strong words to tell you how I felt. I blamed you for so much. I was never able to finish the letters I had started, so I decided to try again. This will be my last correspondence with you.

    I realize I cannot discuss any of this with you since you are resting in your grave, but it does help me to get it off of my chest. I need some closure, but I don't have to be hateful to get my point across. I loved you very much. All I ever wanted was for you to love me too. I've come to terms with the fact that you were broken. We are all broken. I've stopped blaming you, and I've accepted the fact that you did not want me—even on those rare occasions when you may have seemed proud of me or that you might have loved me in some small way. I've tried to see it from your perspective. I've tried to put myself in your shoes to see if I would have felt like you did. It doesn't matter anymore. I have caught myself acting like you for far too long. Though I hated so much of your behavior, I ended up repeating the very same things you modeled to me. I don't want to be like you. I only want to hold onto the good attributes and relinquish the negative ones. You had many flaws, Mom. I'm sure they were handed down to you as well.

    I just want to say good-bye. I want to release you and let you go. I want the God-given power to be myself and no longer allow your opinion of me to overshadow who I really am. I have found myself, and I have my own identity. I am a beautiful, loving wife and mother, and I am worthy of being loved—not just by my husband and children but by anyone who sees value in me. Most of all, I am loved by Jesus. He is my Creator and my Healer, and He sustained me all of these years. I'm sorry, Mom. I'm sorry you had to suffer and be sad and angry for so much of your life. We all have choices and decisions to make. I choose to be happy. I choose to be full of genuine love and compassion.

I can no longer carry the anger and grudges that you have transferred onto me. I cannot help that your dad did some horrific things to you. I've learned through these years of therapy that you damaged me, not because you intentionally did it, but you acted out your anger and hate and projected it onto me. This transference was sick, and my poor little inner child didn't know how to respond to you. So, I shut down. I hid the trauma. I hid the anger. However, when a trigger would come up, so would the anger. I didn't know all these years that you were the cause of this anger, but I know now.

You resented the relationship I had with Daddy. Daddy did NOTHING to me! Yes, he confided in me, yes, he favored me, and yes, he needed an ally. And it was wrong of him to put me in that position. I was too young to have understood, and I don't think he did it deliberately or to be hurtful. He just needed to vent, and I was always available. But he did nothing of a sexual nature to me.

> *I can no longer carry the anger and grudges that you have transferred onto me*

For whatever reason, I felt sorry for him. I was a compassionate child, and he played the pity card very well. I sympathized with him, and it became very easy for me to side with him in most cases. Besides, you always had Becky and Tommy to side with you against him. You both used us kids in very bad ways and put us in positions that we never should have been put in. But you took it a step further. I believe that you took my relationship with Daddy personally. You had an unhealthy jealousy of me, which caused you to treat me in a horrible way. I honestly didn't know what you thought was going on in your sick and twisted mind until my therapist pointed it out. You missed the boat, Mom! You should have been looking at what your sons were doing to your daughters, instead of watching your husband! Daddy was an innocent man who loved you and would have done anything for you. His only guilt was in allowing you to be the head of the house. Yes, I realize now, that his confiding in me was to some degree an emotionally, incestual relationship with his daughter. He expected me to listen and discuss with him the issues he had with you, and that was very wrong of him. I was just a kid; I had no idea what was going on. I certainly do not excuse his behavior or think it was okay in any way. I have forgiven him too for the wrongs against me.

I now know why you were so cruel to me. I reminded you of yourself. You always said that I was the most like you. I didn't want to hear that, Mom! I never wanted to be like you. The truth is, you hated yourself. Because your dad had you locked into some type of incestuous relationship with him, you feared, assumed, or accused (misconstruing in your sick mind) that the same thing was going on with me and Daddy. I had no idea why you hated me. Once I realized, in therapy, that you didn't even want me, that was bad enough. But to realize that you projected your hate of your dad onto me because of your own damage caused me even more pain.

I've come to recognize that my self-loathing came from my lack of love from you. You may have felt the same thing from your own mother. The way your dad treated you likely caused your mom to resent you too, and so the cycle goes. I know you and grandma weren't that close. There was always some hidden pain between you two. Because I was the closest to Daddy, you resented me. You were never as cruel to my siblings as you were to me. Thanks to the therapy I've received, I can accept what happened, and I can forgive you.

I realized you weren't all bad, Mom. You did have some good qualities, and I want to thank you for the morals and values that you instilled in me. Thank you for demonstrating a hard work ethic and a "stick to it" attitude. I am grateful for many things and again, I loved you, at least I loved you as much as I knew how to, considering what little I knew of "love."

I only hope and pray that I will see you again when Jesus returns. I pray that you reconciled all that you needed to with God before your last breath. But if you didn't, that was your choice. We all have to work out our own salvation, and I am not responsible for you. If you prayed for me and really were sincere, then thank you for those prayers.

I am sorry for any pain I caused you over the years. I'm sorry I didn't get to call you and talk to you one last time. It's been twenty years since you died, and I'm done grieving. I forgive you for not wanting me. And I forgive myself for having been born. Rest in peace until Jesus comes.

Love,
Marie, your daughter

I placed the pen gently on my desk and took a deep cleansing breath. It felt as if a huge weight had been lifted. I knew the letter would never be mailed, and I wasn't even sure what I wanted to do with it. I slowly closed the journal and tucked it back into my desk drawer and went to my soft, cozy recliner. I drifted off in thought about the healing that had taken place in my life over the course of the last five years. I realized just how much growth has taken place, and I recognized how much closer I feel to Jesus and my husband through this experience.

If nothing else is taken away from what I've written, I want readers to understand that sometimes it is okay to abandon and forsake family members. Sometimes, in fact, our very own sanity, safety, and ability to thrive is lost if we remain in the toxic dysfunction of our families of origin. Sometimes, our only means of survival is to leave the people completely behind us. Our past will continue to follow us no matter where we go. Thankfully, there is help and healing from the pain and damage that was done to us when we wise up and refuse to allow the abuse to continue by remaining in its grasp. I love them all to this day. I have forgiven every wrong done to me. I have accepted that demonic forces were alive and well in the home atmosphere and that there was a generational curse upon all of us. Every scene from the play of my life had its actors, and every actor had his or her choice in the role they played. I made the choice to get off the stage, to get out of the acting business, and I went to an entirely different theater. God willing, I have stopped the cycle of this curse.

I am living proof that my only means of survival was to leave the city, state, and association of those whom I knew from my infancy on. I was traumatized and abused from the moment I existed. Only God knew what the outcome of my life would be, and, only by surrendering myself to Him could He use me or bring to fruition any plans that He would allow for me. I firmly believe that, had I remained in the family dynamics I knew for forty-three years, I might not even be alive today. I can say with certainty that I would not be the happy, thriving Christian person I am today. There are so many possible scenarios of what would have happened had I taken the optional "fork in the road" in life. Again, only God knows what my outcome would have or could have been had I been left to my own devices. But I made a choice. I listened to that still small voice, and I chose Jesus. I paid attention to the promptings and prodding of the Holy Spirit who was not willing to give up on me. I hung on and believed that there had to be something better for me.

When I was sitting alone in my house, crying in despair and praying that God would help me, I saw no future; I saw nothing beyond my empty life and an unfulfilled job. I had nowhere else to turn. Then, the audible words that I heard in my mind, I believe to this day, were God Himself, speaking to me: "I have so much more in store for you, Marie." I heard Him; I believed Him; and I knew He wanted more for me. I took note of what He said, and I sought Him out. I surrendered all.

Today, I see myself as a very blessed, content Christian woman who desires to serve my Lord and Savior to the best of my ability with His guidance and leading. I know the devil is out there like a roaring lion seeking whom he may devour. But I know that God is bigger and stronger, and, as long as I place myself on His side, He will be there for me. I claim the promise of James 4:7. I will continue to submit myself to the Lord, I will resist the devil, and he will flee. This text has saved my life, and I cling to it.

I am grateful to the medical profession, the therapists, and the medications that helped me get through those very difficult times. I am happy to report, however, that I am no longer taking any prescription medications for anxiety or depression. Through EMDR therapy, I continue to heal, and I have learned coping strategies to apply if and when triggers occur.

I am familiar enough with the devil and his tactics to know that I must run to Jesus in ALL situations! Unfortunately, the devil knows me and my character better than I do; he knows exactly what he can tempt me with; he knows my character flaws and just what he can put in my path to set me off, trip me up, and bring me down. Fortunately, I have a Savior who picks me up, brushes me off, stands me back up straight and tall, and sends me on my way again. He is stronger and mightier than Satan and any of his evil angels. God strengthens me, sooths me, accepts me, but, most of all, He loves me and forgives my stupidity and my ignorance. He knows that I am weak; He knows that I am His child and that I will likely continue to fail in many ways. But He loves me anyway, and my knowing that He loves me makes me want to continue trying to better myself through Him. I want to be filled to the fullest by Him. My desire is to improve the character flaws that I can, but I fully acknowledge that I am helpless without His aid. I want to make better choices and inquire of Him which path He thinks I should take. I just want to be more like Jesus. I want Him to be my teacher, my mentor—not because I am "earning" anything from Him but because I want what He has. I want His mind; I want His emotions; I want His kind of LOVE.

Chapter Notes and "Aha" Moments :

Chapter 16

Final Thoughts from the Author

It occurred to me one morning during my devotions that what I want most out of life is to share my love of Jesus with others. I read about the day of Pentecost and how the first Christians were witnesses for Him. "Go and tell all nations," Jesus said.

How then do I do this? I asked myself. As quickly as the thought came to my mind, the words, *I'm too broken*, popped into my head. I stared into the early morning solitude of my simple home. *What a negative thought that was*, I realized—it was something only the devil would plant. *How can I possibly relate my story?* Negative thoughts hammered home, *You aren't good enough. Who do you think you are?*

God's Word says to love your brethren, "Love one another fervently with a pure heart" (1 Peter 1:22). Any attempts I have made to learn to love have been met by one roadblock after another. When I have thought for sure that I truly loved someone, I would discover that I shouldn't do, say, or think hurtful, unloving things toward that person. Yet, I have found myself doing that very thing—time and time again. In fact, those who genuinely seem to love me take the abuse and seem to love me anyway. This is confusing to me, and why is that? It is because I have struggled hard to understand what love is! All my life, love has eluded me—genuine love, that is.

In my brokenness, I questioned God, "How can such a broken person with as many flaws as I have possibly make a difference in someone else's life? My past is too dark."

It was as if I immediately heard God retort, *But you are healing.* Although stunned at the words I heard in my head, I realized, *It's true, I am healing. But I've got a long way to go, God, and I just don't think I'm good enough!* I argued with that thought, *You don't have to be good enough,* and

Final Thoughts from the Author | 131

then concluded, *I AM good enough!* I believe that the Lord was speaking to me the reassurance I needed. Oftentimes I feel that I am but a child, a damaged child reacting to the pain of my upbringing.

I feel stifled, and, in fact, prior to getting counseling, I was very much a child. I was damaged and acted out of the mindset of a hurt child. Thank God for the promises from the Bible such as 1 Corinthians 13:11, where Paul said: "When I was a child, I spoke as a child, I understood as a child, I thought as a child; but when I became a man (an adult), I put away childish things." Through the healing I am gaining, I am finally able to speak, understand, and think as an adult. I am also able to love as an adult now and not function from my childhood brokenness. I truly can be a witness for Jesus!

We are all broken people, and those who are seeking to be healed will find healing if we only seek the Lord with an earnest, surrendered, and sincere heart. As for me, I don't know how much more healing I need to experience. I can't help but believe that healing is a lifelong endeavor, and God can still use me. This is the process of sanctification; we are all being sanctified with each new day as long as we make ourselves available and willing. If we ever reach the point that we believe we've "made it," we had better be worried. There are so many examples in the Bible of those who walked close to Jesus still making mistakes. They too were a work in progress.

Because of God's wonderful grace, I am now better able to see myself as the adult person God intended me to be, not the person I was trained to be from infancy—a person who had horrible role models and dysfunctional, irrational behaviors to learn from

Every day I am seeing progress, and the flaws in my character are becoming more of a memory than an occurrence. Because of God's wonderful grace, I am now better able to see myself as the adult person God intended me to be, not the person I was trained to be from infancy—a person who had horrible role models and dysfunctional, irrational behaviors to learn from. The truth is, we all have a story. Every one of us could be witnessing to our neighbors, friends, co-workers, and others of the wonderful ways that God has brought us through one trial after another.

Oh, how I wish I could have had a different beginning, but I didn't. And now, as I learn more about myself and where I've come from, I am becoming so grateful to realize that God truly loves me and sees value in me, and I realize that my story of survival can benefit others as they journey to find wholeness in Jesus. The fact is, Jesus has been with me through it all. He has guided and protected me even in times when I didn't know that I needed His help.

My journey of healing and wholeness continues on, and, as long as there is progress, I am unstoppable. Frequently my defects of character are being brought to my awareness through the work of the Holy Spirit, and, as long as I keep asking Him to reveal them to me, He will. It is up to me then to repent of these flaws and surrender them over to His power daily and hourly, if necessary, until I have conquered them through His divine power. All of the glory be to God.

In the same way, in dealing with my addiction to cigarettes and alcohol, I had to have the desire to stop these harmful habits. Only then was I able to surrender them over to God. My addiction to hate, my resentment, my criticism and negativity are simply addictions and bad habits. I don't want to do, say, or think as I do, yet I fall into the same patterns over and over, and then I beat myself up for what I have done, said, or thought time and time again. Overwhelmed with guilt, I sink into a pile of gooey self-pity and either I sulk or, even worse, I get bitter, angry, resentful, critical, and negative. And so the cycle goes. Perhaps it is that sometimes we don't want to stop these habits. They are, after all, part of our identity. Some of these flaws are hereditary and part of our DNA. Other flaws come from being trained and from having these bad traits modeled for us as children, which means that they are all we have ever known. Such defects of character need to be unlearned.

Is it possible that we have to ask God to give us the desire to sever these character flaws? Perhaps this is one of the steps to recovery. In order to work through the process of getting rid of our defects of character, we have to recognize how damaging they are to those we come in contact with. We must possess a desire to change that is so strong that we begin to detest these character defects. After all, we don't like these flaws in other people, and we are quick to spot them, point them out, and judge the people for having them. Yet, many of us are okay allowing bad behaviors in our own characters. With God's help, I feel "unstoppable," though He makes it possible for me to "stop" the bad in my life, so those things *are* stoppable. He has replaced the bad that Satan intended for my ruin, and He puts in me His desires, His character traits, and His love.

I've reached the point of seeing the "despicable me," and I don't like her. My desire in life is now to be the kind of person that people genuinely love and want to be around, the kind of person Jesus was—consistent in His behavior. I don't want to be "wishy-washy." I don't want to doubt and be like the waves of the sea as the Bible describes in James 1:6–8. I want to have faith and not to be double-minded and unstable in my ways. I want to claim the promises of Philippians 1:6: "Being confident of this very thing, that He who has begun a good work in [me] will complete it until the day of Jesus Christ."

I'll never forget when I decided to seek help from a professional therapist. I felt a hollow void in my life. I was told that it is very difficult to love anyone else until I can genuinely love myself.

"Do you feel loved?"

I let that question sink in for a few seconds, and then I fell apart like a sugar cube dissolving in a teaspoon of water. The reality all came to me in a matter of seconds, and the lie that I had believed for over fifty years hit me right between the eyes, going right to my brain and heart at the same time. The floodgates opened, and out came the truth.

My therapist asked me to think back to my earliest recollection of feeling loved, nurtured, and cared for, and that is what brought about the need to write and share my story. It was not so I could run down and criticize my family of origin, and it certainly was not to gain sympathy. I chose to write about my life so that I could help others who have battled with "love" or the lack thereof. The reality is that the love I received in my childhood home was conditional love. If I was good enough, if I cleaned the house well enough, if I obeyed, and if I was the perfect little girl, then I could receive the attention I so desperately craved. This attention is what I, as a little girl equated with love. But, heaven forbid, if I messed up at all, the love was withheld, and I was ignored, chastised, neglected, and hated. What a traumatic, frightening reality for a child who so desperately wanted a mother's love! It wasn't just that I wasn't loved; it was that I had to face and accept the reality that I was horribly abused! My entire identity of who I believed myself to be began while I was a fetus with the guilt of even being born. Then repeated pronouncement, "Shame on you!" or "You should be ashamed of yourself!" crushed the life out of "little Marie." After all, guilt comes about from something bad *we've done* (or think we've done), but shame is something that makes us feel bad for *who we are*. My very identity was one of feeling guilty for being born, feeling shame for having even existed.

The desire to share my story of learning to love myself based on God's word is critical to me. I also have a burning desire to expose Satan for who he is. I want readers to understand why he is so determined to not only destroy God's character, but he wants to get to the very heart of our identity. The way we see ourselves from God's perspective is the key to our being able to love ourselves so that we can genuinely love others.

We must realize that God's love is unconditional. We must never ask "am I good enough?" or "Did I do enough?" The devil wants us to feel that we must earn this love. We don't! Jesus' love was so great that he died a cruel death on the cross which paid the price for us. We only have to accept this free gift. Jesus wants us to love ourselves and see the value in ourselves and why we were worth dying for. This is the love that He sees in us. The valuable love He wants us to have for ourselves.

> *The desire to share my story of learning to love myself based on God's word is critical to me. I also have a burning desire to expose Satan for who he is*

I'm not referring to arrogant, narcissistic love of self. I am talking about being able to look in the mirror, look into our eyes, and see the depths of our own being, to say to ourselves, "God loves me, God wanted me to be born, and He has a purpose for me. I want to give myself a hug and say to myself, 'I love you.' And I want to say and believe it with my mind, heart, and soul!

I am the wife of a pastor, and, after years of trying to force myself to be happy, I came to realize I needed outside help. God's Word alone could not shed the light on my deeper issues. Yet, now that I understand more clearly that God's Word is vital to the remainder of my healing process, I have never needed God and His Word more than I do now.

I appreciate being able to share my painful story and to conclude with hope, reconciliation, and a future full of ongoing healing and love—yes, love that I continue to learn about—such as the love for the brethren that Peter described: "Love one another fervently with a pure heart, having been born again, not of corruptible seed but incorruptible, through the word of God which lives and abides forever" (1 Peter 1:22, 23). I am learning to love—God first, then me. Perhaps love will flow out of me as God intended it to all along. I want to be the most loving wife, mother, friend, and neighbor that I can be. It is my goal to uplift and glorify my Lord and Creator. I have no idea what the future holds, but I do know that I want God to hold my future. If God is exalted and even one person finds solace in my story, then it has been worth it all. Each person who reads my story will prayerfully come away with the awareness that he or she is also valuable to God, despite what your dysfunctional family of origin may have told you. Some parts of my story will no doubt resonate more with some readers than others.

I truly wish I could say that reconciliation occurred within my family, but the reconciliation I refer to is that in my own mind and heart. I have found forgiveness for all that was done to me, and I have chosen to leave the past where it belongs—in the past. Many of my abusers are long gone and resting in their graves. Those who are still alive will obviously have a different perspective, based on their own perception of the events that took place. I can only speak the truth from my experience and my own perception, my own reality of what happened. I recently heard someone say, "The past is not the past if it is still affecting your present." So, even though I will always have "triggers" and reminders of my past, it is how I choose to respond to those reminders that truly shows the growth I am making toward ultimate healing. I thank God for bringing me through the trials that I've had to overcome, and I now choose to live in the present. I pray that God will bless you today and always and abundantly with healing and genuine, unconditional love. I firmly believe that God brought me to EMDR therapy. I believe that, without it, I would not be where I am today. I have gone from **having a "God hole" to being in God Whole**, and I continue to encourage people to seek help. I forewarn you to pray diligently for the right therapist, and God will lead you to the one you need to find healing. I believe I am well on my way. I want you, too, to have the same kind of wholeness. May you listen to Him and respond to His calling that you too can go "From God Hole to God Whole." This is my prayer for you! Amen.

Be blessed,
Marie

Chapter Notes and "Aha" Moments :

TEACH Services, Inc.
P U B L I S H I N G

We invite you to view the complete
selection of titles we publish at:
www.TEACHServices.com

We encourage you to write us
with your thoughts about this,
or any other book we publish at:
info@TEACHServices.com

TEACH Services' titles may be purchased in
bulk quantities for educational, fund-raising,
business, or promotional use.
bulksales@TEACHServices.com

Finally, if you are interested in seeing
your own book in print, please contact us at:
publishing@TEACHServices.com
We are happy to review your manuscript at no charge.